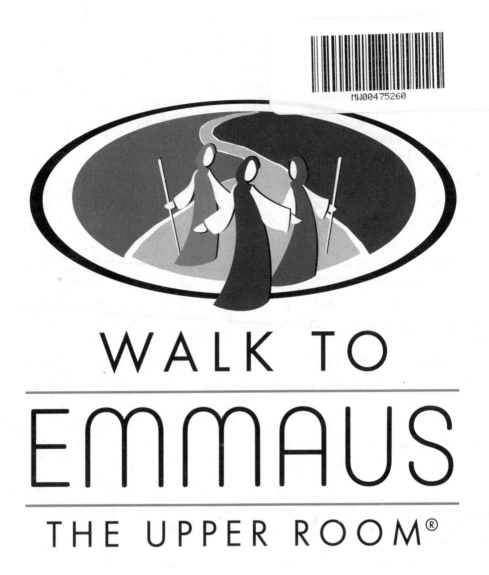

WALK TO
EMMAUS
THE UPPER ROOM®

TEAM MANUAL

UPPER
ROOM BOOKS®
NASHVILLE

Cover design: Tim Green | Faceout Studio
Interior design: PerfecType, Nashville, TN

Print ISBN 978-0-8358-1769-1
Mobi ISBN 978-0-8358-1770-7
Epub ISBN 978-0-8358-1771-4

Printed in the United States of America

**For more information about The Walk to Emmaus
or to learn about other Emmaus Ministries resources**
see emmaus.upperroom.org/
or call the International Emmaus Ministries Office
at (877) 899-2780 ext.7113 or (615) 340-7113.

CONTENTS

WALK TO EMMAUS TEAM CANON

IT'S NOT ABOUT ME!

- I am a member of an Emmaus team; therefore, I am only one part of a complete being.
- I am an imperfect earthen vessel, and I am blessed to be here in a servant's role.
- I will serve in humility and gratitude for the opportunity to be here and will remember that the Holy Spirit calls for my love, patience, kindness, gentleness, and self-control in all things.
- I will pray for submission to the Holy Spirit and for strength and commitment to be God's person rather than my own person during this time.
- I will remember that I am here only as an instrument through which God can work to renew the church.
- I am here only by God's grace and only so that the Holy Spirit might work through me.
- I will lift up other team members and pilgrims in prayer and ask our Lord to strengthen them and open their eyes so that we all might recognize Jesus Christ in the breaking of the bread.
- I will not overstate or overemphasize my role by any word or deed.
- I will not glorify myself; I will not glorify any other team member nor allow another to glorify me.
- I will remember that the pilgrims are the main reason for my presence and my prayers.
- I will remember at all times that I am no more important than any other person with whom I am sharing this experience.
- In all things, I will accept and obey the authority and discipline under which I serve.
- I have no authority or responsibility except to obey God and to respond to the ministry of the Holy Spirit.
- Whatever passions and excitement seize me, I will express them through joyful praise to God, my Lord Jesus Christ, and the Holy Spirit.
- I will give God all the glory for whatever happens during this time together.

- I will raise my voice only to praise God and will bow my head in reverence and submission to God.

- I am only a servant, but God can use me more powerfully in this role than in any other role I might choose.

- I am a member of an Emmaus team; in all things, I pray that Christ will be lifted up.

SECTION 1—
THE EMMAUS MINISTRIES FAMILY

PURPOSE

Emmaus Ministries exists to inspire, challenge, and equip local faith communities for Christian action in their homes, churches, communities, and places of work. This purpose does not come to full realization for its pilgrims during the Emmaus Ministries event itself but in the many days that follow.

Emmaus Ministries expands pilgrims' spiritual lives, deepens their faith and discipleship, and rekindles—or perhaps ignites for the first time—their gifts as Christian leaders for their churches and communities. These aims are accomplished not only during the Emmaus Ministries event itself but also through participation in follow-up spiritual support groups and Community fellowship opportunities, sponsorship, prayer, support of other Emmaus Ministries events, and service on support committees and on teams.

Persons whose spiritual lives are renewed and strengthened through Emmaus Ministries are called and empowered to be the hands and feet of Christ: to share within their communities the grace they received. They become energetic and renewing catalysts in their homes, places of work or education, and local communities of faith. While walking together with other Christians, they actively participate in God's mission to the world.

HISTORY AND SCOPE

Emmaus Ministries includes programs for those seeking spiritual formation in several different life-stages:

- **Chrysalis** serves secondary (high school) young persons fifteen to eighteen years old;
- **Journey to the Table** serves young adults eighteen to thirty-five years old;
- **Walk to Emmaus** serves adults eighteen years and older;
- **Face to Face** serves adults sixty years and older.

Origins of the Ministries

Traditionally, in Christianity, a "three-day movement" was a movement that conducted spiritual renewal events and led by persons who had attended such an event. All such organizations were often collectively referred to as "three-day movements."

Most, but not all, of the events held by these organizations covered three days, and so the *fourth day* has become a term used by three-day movements to describe the life of the pilgrim after the event.

The original three-day movement, Cursillo (cur-SEE-yoh), began in the Roman Catholic Church in Majorca, Spain, in 1944. Over time, Cursillo inspired the development of the Emmaus Ministries family of "three-day movement" programs.

Several resources provide information about the history of the Emmaus three-day movement and its relationship to Cursillo: *Day Four: The Pilgrim's Continued Journey*, *What Is Emmaus?*, and *The Early History of the Walk to Emmaus*.

In 1976, Danny Morris, Director of Developing Ministries for The Upper Room, participated in a Lutheran Cursillo in Florida and recognized the need for an ecumenical offering of Cursillo. On the same weekend, Maxie Dunnam, then World Editor of The Upper Room, participated in a prayer retreat at First United Methodist Church in Peoria, Illinois, where Cursillo pilgrims served as table servants at the retreat. Their spiritual presence about the tables profoundly affected him.

Together, Danny and Maxie began to take steps toward including Cursillo as an Upper Room program. Under the leadership of Reverend Robert Wood, The Upper Room's first two model Cursillo weekends were held in Peoria, Illinois, in 1977. In 1978, Rev. Wood joined the staff of The Upper Room to launch the new Upper Room Cursillo movement.

In 1981, by mutual agreement with the National Secretariat of the Roman Catholic Cursillo, holder of the copyright to the Cursillo program, The Upper Room Cursillo became The Upper Room Walk to Emmaus. This change came about due to The Upper Room's call to be an ecumenical movement. The Upper Room reached an agreement with the National Cursillo Secretariat to develop a new program based on Cursillo but with distinctive leadership resources. Further, The Upper Room agreed not to use the traditional Cursillo language derived from its Spanish origin. The Upper Room developed The Walk to Emmaus design, talk outlines, and leadership manuals for use by an ecumenical audience.

Chrysalis began in 1984 in response to numerous requests from Emmaus Ministries Communities for a version of the Walk to Emmaus specifically for high school students. The Walk to Emmaus and TEC (Teens Encounter Christ—the youth expression of the Roman Catholic Cursillo) influenced the early development of Chrysalis. A group of Nashville high school youth attended TEC and acted as advisers to The Upper Room staff in creating a unique model and name for the program. And then, in 1989, The Upper Room and the Alabama/West Florida Emmaus Community sponsored the first Chrysalis event for college-age young people.

Face to Face, an adaptation of The Walk to Emmaus, was developed to meet the needs and life stages of older adults and those for whom an overnight experience presented a challenge.

Development of the Face to Face program began in 2008, with the first Encounter being held in 2011 in a Nashville area church. In 2014, the first Encounter using the officially developed materials took place and in 2015 Emmaus Ministries Communities outside the Nashville area began to hold Encounters.

Journey to the Table had its beginning in March of 2014, when The Upper Room established a new staff position for "Young Adult Spiritual Development." In September of 2014, the first five steering team leaders came to Nashville for three days of prayerful discussion and planning. After that meeting, an additional fourteen people joined working groups to write the first draft of the program. This group included young adults, campus ministers, and Emmaus and Chrysalis leaders. That draft of the new Journey to the Table program was completed in March of 2015, and five locations held test events in 2015 and 2016. The official launch of the program was held at The Upper Room in Nashville, Tennessee, in July 2016.

SECTION 2—
OVERVIEW

The exciting adventure of becoming a Conference Room Team member requires your preparation for service through prayer. Spending daily time with God, following the pattern of the Emmaus accountability group card, and participating regularly in your accountability group provide the foundation for effective team membership. It helps you focus your study on topics related to team formation and your role on the team.

Several Upper Room publications serve as resources for the Emmaus event, including this *Team Manual.* A valuable resource related to your understanding of service is the book *Celebration of Discipline* by Richard Foster. In chapter 9, titled "The Discipline of Service," Foster states, "If true service is to be understood and practiced it must be distinguished clearly from 'self-righteous service'" (Harper & Row 1978, 111).

The lifelong experience of the Walk to Emmaus begins with a short course in Christianity. God—working through the team members—directs the pilgrims, encouraging greater involvement and accountability as disciples of Jesus Christ.

During the Walk to Emmaus pilgrims active within the church come to understand better their commitment to the vows taken for them or accepted by them at the time of their baptism. Someone once said the Walk to Emmaus was like "the joyful communication of being Christian." Simply put, the walk represents what it means to be a true disciple of Jesus Christ in the world.

The primary focus of Emmaus is the local church where ministry takes place. The objective of this Walk to Emmaus is to inspire, motivate, challenge, and equip local church members for Christian action in their home, church, work, and community.

During the Walk to Emmaus, God will use you and the other team members to help pilgrims

1. grow in their individual spiritual lives,
2. become more effective disciples of Jesus Christ in the world through their local churches, and
3. engage actively in God's mission to the world.

The renewal of the church will come about as laypersons and clergy intentionally work together. The immense task of renewal requires all our efforts.

GENERAL PRINCIPLES

Our Lord commands us to "Go into all the world and proclaim the good news to the whole creation" (Mark 16:15). Emmaus depends on the life experiences of others, both lay and clergy, to assist in bringing about a spiritual renewal. Only then may persons return from their Walk to Emmaus prepared to witness to others and to bring these others to an understanding of the saving grace in Jesus Christ. The Walk to Emmaus relies wholly on those who respond to the call of Christ in their life to be this witness during the Walk. This team is the primary instrument in and through which the Holy Spirit works to affect the lives of those who attend. Thus, our faith and what occurs during this time rest not on us but on the power of the Holy Spirit working in and through us. (See 1 Corinthians 2:4-5.)

Much of what happens during the Walk fosters the removal of obstacles or barriers that keep pilgrims from a close relationship with God. God uses the team members during the Walk to Emmaus to prepare the way, so the pilgrims experience renewal to serve God. ("In the wilderness prepare the way of the LORD, make straight in the desert a highway for our God" [Isa. 40:3].)

The design of Emmaus tries to provide an atmosphere in which persons feel free to experience once again, or perhaps for the first time, their relationship with the risen Christ. It affords an opportunity to demonstrate the unconditional love of God who accepts the pilgrims for whom and whose they are.

The Walk to Emmaus design offers a step-by-step approach to biblical truths through talks given by lay and clergy, which moves the pilgrims to decide consciously to open themselves more fully to God. However, remember that Emmaus is not for everyone. While many will respond in a positive way to this Emmaus experience, some will not. Respect for individual choice remains fundamental to the success of Emmaus. This respect for choice will allow the team to offer pilgrims the vision of what the Christian life can be.

The Walk to Emmaus embraces the following attitudes, actions, and qualities:

- faithful adherence to The Upper Room model;
- continual openness to the leading of the Holy Spirit;
- genuine attention given to pilgrims' needs;
- humble offering of the fifteen talks by lay and clergy speakers;
- ongoing prayer.

Prayer is the principal means to any successful Emmaus event. The Emmaus Community, friends, family, the Lay Director, the Spiritual Director, and team members pray earnestly before and during the Walk for God to use this time to bring others to a closer relationship with God. Jesus said, "Where two or three are gathered in my name, I am there among them" (Matt. 18:20). After walking to Emmaus, the two disciples sat at table with Jesus and broke bread, and "their eyes were opened" (Luke 24:31). The Community of believers prays that the pilgrims' eyes will be opened during the Walk to Emmaus.

Those who participate, pilgrims and team members alike, draw their inspiration to pray from the Holy Spirit. First Thessalonians 4:8 reminds us, "God . . . gives his Holy Spirit to you." May that same Holy Spirit give us wisdom and encouragement to be led as we lead others.

SECTION 3—THE WALK TO EMMAUS TEAM

You have been asked to serve on a team for a Walk to Emmaus weekend. This privilege brings both honor and humility. Your participation will call for a commitment to the spiritual growth of the team and to the discipline required of a successful team member. It will also call for many hours of work, and you will discover the great effort that went into the preparation for your Emmaus weekend. The privilege of serving on a team requires personal discipline, sacrifice, and obedience to the authority of the Lay and Spiritual Directors of the weekend.

Every person who contributes to the Emmaus weekend for which you are a team member is equally important and valuable. The person who will pray at 3:00 a.m. on each of the three days for you and the pilgrims or the one who will mop the kitchen floor is as vital to this ministry as are the team members who have direct contact with the pilgrims.

In a spirit of love and with high idealism, let your preparations for the weekend carry you forward to the glory of God.

TEAM SELECTION

Emmaus and Face to Face pilgrims, as well as adult Chrysalis butterflies, compose a Walk to Emmaus team. Team members bring a broad range of God-given talents and gifts to glorify God, build up God's reign, and renew the church. Within this spectrum of individuals, *all* team members share commitment to Christian discipleship, church renewal, and apostolic action.

Given that a person affirms this basic commitment, another weighty consideration in team selection includes participation in the following Fourth Day activities:

- Regular church attendance;
- Involvement in a local church;
- Support of Emmaus Gatherings;
- Ongoing participation in an accountability group;
- Servanthood ministry behind the scenes of Emmaus events.

THE SPIRIT OF EMMAUS

The spirit in which an Emmaus ministry event is conducted is none other than the Holy Spirit.

In Galatians 5:22-26, the apostle Paul lists "the fruit of the Spirit," characteristics of the Holy Spirit manifested in people's attitudes and behavior. This fruit represents the character of a team properly formed in the spirit of Jesus Christ. We want pilgrims to feast on this fruit throughout their event. The fruit of the Spirit serves as a good backdrop for describing team attitudes and practices. Team leaders can cultivate among team members a readiness to embrace the quality of community life that the Holy Spirit brings by reviewing one aspect of the fruit of the Spirit at each team meeting.

Love

An atmosphere of hospitality and acceptance characterizes the weekend Community. The team promotes the feeling of an open and opportune space for pilgrims to respond freely and honestly to the gospel of grace in the presence of people who care, a time in which the pilgrims can rediscover themselves in relationship with God. The environment of unconditional love allows people to lower their defenses and allows God to touch their lives with grace. The team motto for Kairos (the prison ministry expression of Cursillo) suits Emmaus equally well: "listen, listen, love, love."

However, this love draws attention to God—not to team members. An ancient image depicts the spiritual life as a wagon wheel with spokes connecting at the center. The center represents God in Jesus Christ, and the wheel rim represents people. As we turn and move toward the center, we, at the same time, draw closer to one another. When we attempt to move closer to one another along the rim of human need and natural inclination, we do not necessarily move closer to God. Nor do we necessarily move closer to lasting, spiritual relationships with one another. Emmaus attempts to turn people's attention toward God and draw them closer to God. This process then draws pilgrims together as spiritual friends into a Christian community of the Holy Spirit's making.

The wagon wheel image of the spiritual life reminds the team members that their behavior calls attention to God, not to themselves. The image also reminds the team that God's presence does not result from human togetherness or a feeling of human closeness. Team members need not take action that they believe will accelerate feelings of intimacy or push pilgrims to share beyond their levels of willingness. God will draw the pilgrims together as they turn their attention to God's welcoming love and as their hearts overflow with the gift of that love in the company of one another. On the Walk, pilgrims will experience how the grace of God in Jesus Christ draws people together into a new community of the Holy Spirit's own creation, a community centered in the freedom of God's love rather than in the egoism and neediness intrinsic to human love.

Joy

A Walk has many occasions of true joy: the joy of singing, the joy of self-expression or uninhibited laughter, the joy of insight, the joy of liberation from the shackles of sin or inner hurt or murderous anger, the joy of knowing God's presence, the joy of feeling accepted, and the joy of giving one's life wholeheartedly and without reservation to Jesus Christ. The joy of Emmaus comes in moments of seriousness and in moments of great fun. In all of these ways, team members, as well as the pilgrims, experience the joy of the Lord and of life together in Christian community. They let their joy be known in song, sharing, and enthusiasm for the Christian ideal. The team can set the tone for the Walk through an attitude of joyful anticipation of the Lord's coming to each person in some real, though unforeseen, way along the road.

The team takes care that the expression of joy in fun does not give way to boisterousness and getting carried away: allowing jokes to get out of hand or letting people go too far in making fun of one another. Extroverts—pilgrims or team members—can take over the weekend in such a way that introverts feel left out and do not participate. During the fun time of sharing summaries and the various representations in the evenings, laughter and hilarity may totally overshadow and render pointless the recap of the day's talks and the sharing of each table's insights. The team and pilgrims can have fun while also showing appreciation and sensitivity toward the thoughts and creativity expressed at each table.

Getting carried away also occurs when negative traditions such as "stealing the bell" and the amusement this creates for a few disrupts weekends for all. Stealing the bell is a tradition among team members who feel a need to make the Walk livelier. Team members' attempts to create more fun result from insecurity about the adequacy of the Walk, a desire to make sure the pilgrims have the experience they themselves had on their Walk, or perhaps boredom and a need to make the Walks more exciting for themselves. Team members, especially team leaders, remain aware of the team's influence on the atmosphere of the Walk and share concerns in the nightly team meetings.

Peace

People who walk in the Spirit enjoy the fruit of peace with God and one another. Team members exhibit conscious care for their relationship with God and other people and practice the peace that comes from faith in God's love and direction. Then team members enjoy the inner security of being only themselves on Walks. They need not act more spiritual than usual, more religious than others, or make a perfect report on their Christian life and home. However, team members actively strive to practice their piety, study, and action and want to live an authentic Christian life. Team members who feel they must work to maintain an image or who pretend to uphold a way of life that they have never practiced will find no peace.

Peace also comes from faith in God's love for all people. Pilgrims in Emmaus come from many denominations, races, and walks of life. They may differ considerably in their views on doctrine, church, politics, and the world. They find themselves at different levels of Christian maturity and experience. Yet, despite their differences, team members share the peace of

Christ with the pilgrims and foster community among them by modeling Christian tolerance and charity toward all.

Christian tolerance does not imply indifference toward sound Christian belief and theology. It does mean focusing on the common essentials of Christian faith while not letting differences over doctrine become more powerful than the love of Christ in relationships. The team's attitude is as follows: If your heart is as my heart, then give me your hand. (See 2 Kings 10:15.) Emmaus attempts to set forth the essentials of Christian faith and practice that characterize the mainstream of Christian tradition, the gift of God's peace indeed "surpasses all understanding" (Phil. 4:7).

Team members do not set the pilgrims straight on details of doctrine. Rather, they "love, love; listen, listen," leaving the rest to God and trusting the process of the weekend. When differences over belief arise among pilgrims, team members challenge them to affirm the gift in each other's perspectives, to explore those beliefs more fully with their pastors when they return home, and to stay focused on the message and experience of the Walk.

Team members are always the first to extend the hand of Christian fellowship. "Let peace begin with me" becomes their personal motto and prayer. The team can foster the peace of Christ among the pilgrims by modeling an open and nondefensive spirit, by speaking the truth in love, and by being quick to forgive or say, "I'm sorry." The team members keep in mind that they have been given the peace of Christ so they can pass that peace to others. This peace comes from a vital relationship with God.

Patience

A Walk is a full but slow walk with the Lord. Even though the pilgrims follow the same path, each experience is unique. The pilgrims hear and see the Lord in their own way, according to their needs and God's will for them at the time of the Walk. Team members guard against the temptation to run ahead of the pilgrims, to hurry them toward their meaningful moment along the way or to rob them of their own experience by previewing upcoming scenes: "Wait until you see what's going to happen next!"

Working on a team requires patience—not only with the pilgrims but also with the work of the Lord in the process. A definition of functional atheism is the belief operative in people who profess God but whose lifestyle reflects an assumption that nothing will happen unless they make it happen themselves. Team members are functional atheists when they try to do God's work for God, try to speed up the movement of the Holy Spirit, try to "save" the pilgrims or bring them to a "decision" or manipulate an emotionally charged atmosphere. God transforms the pilgrims; team members simply love them, openly share their own faith stories and witness, and give the pilgrims space to explore their relationship with God among people who care and listen.

One pilgrim bore witness to the power of patience on the part of the team. After what was for him a life-changing event, he remarked, "What really surprised me was that the team members at my table were not putting anything over on me. They didn't make me feel I was bad or wrong because I didn't see things their way or have an experience with God like theirs.

I felt free to respond honestly the whole time, and I did. About midway I was overcome by the enormous love behind the whole weekend and what was for me an experience of God. I can't believe I'm saying this, but for the first time in my life I think I know what it means to say I know Jesus."

The patience of this pilgrim's Table Leaders and team leaders gave him freedom to experience the Walk in his own way. They trusted the process. Team members can trust the Holy Spirit to touch the pilgrims' lives through the scheduled activities and interactions of the Walk-in ways that may or may not be outwardly evident.

Sometimes team members, more than the pilgrims, need not anticipate. Leadership also stresses that team members expect no formulaic response from the pilgrims, that each person's response to the Walk will be individual. While true in theory, individual response is not true in practice unless team members let go of their expectations for the Walk and replace them with a prayer of thanksgiving for God's grace already at work in each pilgrim's life. They open the way by giving themselves as open and caring instruments for the fulfillment of God's purpose in God's own time in each pilgrim's life.

Team members display patience when they allow the pilgrims to have their own experience and honor the different places pilgrims find themselves on their spiritual journeys. Team members show patience when they relinquish the presumption of knowing what the pilgrims really need and trust God to touch each one in a unique way. Team members exhibit patience when their manner communicates respect for the pilgrims' spiritual integrity, thus making the Walk an accepting space where they feel free to respond authentically to God's presence. Team members employ patience when they trust the process of Emmaus and the sovereign power of grace in people's lives.

Kindness

Kindness is love expressed in specific acts of caring, attention, and undeserved charity. The pilgrims experience the kindness of God through the attention of the team and the Emmaus Community to the pilgrims' every need and through the extraordinarily detailed care that makes Emmaus a special gift. Saint Augustine once wrote about God, *"You are good and all-powerful, caring for each one of us as though the only one in your care"* (Augustine, *Confessions*, trans. Henry Chadwick [Oxford: Oxford University Press, 2009], 3.11.19, 50). This is the kind of love we hope the pilgrims will experience through the kindness of the team and Community. A pilgrim, a United Methodist District Superintendent, once described his experience of a Walk as "three days of Christian affirmation."

Team members set out to acknowledge, converse with, involve, affirm, serve, and pray for the pilgrims so that they may know their value as persons and as citizens of God's reign. Another pilgrim noted, "In every phase of my life, I am in charge. I am constantly giving. One of the hardest things on the Walk for me was letting someone else be in charge and allowing myself to learn again to receive, not only from people but from God." Emmaus frees the pilgrims from their need to control so they can receive and experience the grace of God's love for who they are, rather than for what or how much they can do.

Emmaus is an extraordinary act of God's kindness. Few programs involve the investment of so much from so many for the sake of so few. Team members take care that kindness does not turn into control. Pilgrims do not experience God's kindness when the team's attention becomes smothering watchfulness. While the communal and scheduled nature of Emmaus requires that the team leaders do the best they can to keep the pilgrims on the evenly paced schedule, they do this with kindness, sensitivity, and respect.

Team and Community helpers do not call attention to their acts of kindness, even in the Closing. The Lay Director may recognize the persons who have contributed to the weekend so that the pilgrims have the opportunity to express their gratitude. However, it is contrary to the spirit of Emmaus for the Lay or Spiritual Director to pour enormous praise upon the team and Community helpers or to single out specific members for applause. Closing's focus remains on the pilgrims and God's work in their lives.

Pilgrims are always treated with kindness and respect—never treated poorly or unfairly on any Walk for any reason. In some rare aberrations, in the early days of Cursillo and its spin-offs, pilgrims were treated coldly by the team and were served meager, distasteful portions at mealtimes early in the weekend in order to simulate the dramatic contrast between the life in the world versus the abundance of life and grace in Christian community. This approach has no place in Emmaus. A Walk is real life in Christian community for a time. The team members are not actors who play the roles of cold and then caring persons; they must be real people, striving to live in grace with their neighbor during the Walk. Pilgrims do not need to be shown the way life is in the world through such methods; they already know all too well the patterns and problems of life and their need for grace. That is why they want to experience the Walk to Emmaus.

Goodness

A fruit of being grafted to the true vine of Jesus Christ is the goodness of God's self-giving and sacrificial love. Jesus said, "No one is good but God alone" (Mark 10:18). Jesus embodied the fullness of God's goodness in selfless love and humble servanthood.

"Let the same mind be in you that was in Christ Jesus, who, though he was in the form of God, did not regard equality with God as something to be exploited, but emptied himself, taking the form of a slave, being born in human likeness. And being found in human form, he humbled himself and became obedient to the point of death—even death on a cross" (Phil. 2:5-8).

Jesus, through his sacrificial love, gave up his advantage *over* human beings to become an advantage *to* them; he surrendered his divine credentials to live without distinction as a human among humans, thereby bringing God's grace to them. Jesus, as a humble servant called attention to God not himself. He accomplished what he did under authority, not of his own accord. He did not belong to himself; he was the healing hands and saving Word of God. His success was God's success; he found his reward in God's glory.

The team and Emmaus Community are to manifest the same spirit of selfless love and humble servanthood. In fact, team members and the Community understand their responsibilities for the Walk as spiritual exercises in selfless love and Christian servanthood. Team members' own need for affirmation and attention, while real, is cared for during the weekly team meeting prior to the Walk and during the nightly team meetings during the Walk.

Faithfulness

Each Walk depends on the team members' faithfulness to God, to team leaders, to The Upper Room Emmaus model, and to the pilgrims. When persons accept the call to serve on an Emmaus team, they enter into an implicit covenant with God and the Emmaus Community to make the best Walk possible for the pilgrims. This covenant involves an agreement to serve under the direction of the appointed Lay and Spiritual Directors of the team and to support their leadership wholeheartedly during team formation and during the Walk. It also involves an agreement by team leaders and members to abide faithfully by the purpose and procedures of The Upper Room Emmaus Ministries.

Team members keep faith with one another by attending team meetings, praying for one another during team formation, and helping one another prepare for talks or other responsibilities. The team keeps faith with the Lay and Spiritual Directors by respecting their personal and team schedules, being prepared for assignments at team meetings, praying for their strength and wisdom to lead, honoring their authority, and being their friend throughout.

Team members, leaders, and the Board of Directors keep faith with The Upper Room Emmaus Ministries and the Emmaus movement by following the Emmaus manuals and outlines—a responsibility particularly incumbent upon the Lay and Spiritual Directors of each Walk. This commitment to the program's intent assures the quality of the Emmaus experience being offered and its continuity with Emmaus across the rest of the movement as a trusted instrument of Christian renewal. The manuals represent the objective standards and procedures for Emmaus, the common ground upon which a team can grow in a shared understanding of what Emmaus is and how to conduct it properly.

Team members also keep faith with the pilgrims—first, through fidelity to the aims of The Upper Room Emmaus Ministries, second, by being a true spiritual friend. We all need people who see Christ in us. Team members help the pilgrims claim the promise in their lives and affirm their gifts. They support the pilgrims' desire to live their lives to the fullest in grace. Team members keep faith by holding confidences as well. Finally, team members keep faith with the pilgrims *after* the weekend by following up on friendships that developed during the Walk; holding the pilgrims in prayer, writing to them, helping them develop accountability groups and participate in church, and showing them in every way possible that their Walk experience was real.

Gentleness

The highly-structured nature of a Walk requires gentleness from its leadership. A regimented approach to the Walk is antithetical to the spirit of Emmaus. A Walk is a long and renewing stroll not a forced march. Team members exercise discipline in their leadership, and their motivation for discipline is care for the pilgrims' ultimate experience during the Walk. Though leaders want to enlist the complete participation of every pilgrim on every step of the journey, they need not be overbearing or controlling; it is a matter of attitude and style. A commanding or belittling style *works against* the pilgrims' desire to cooperate and demonstrates that team members have not appropriated the grace they talk about. A gentle and respectful approach *works with* the pilgrims' desire to cooperate and their freedom to be there. Such an approach communicates care for persons and for the program and conveys the grace of the Lord's companionship on the Walk.

Persons who exercise gentleness in leadership conduct the Walk with firmness *and* flexibility. The team is both firm and confident with the pilgrims about the value of each part of the Emmaus experience and the kind of participation being asked of them. The team members also respond with flexibility when needed. Even if the entire Walk is technically flawless, the experience will fall short of being a means of grace to pilgrims who experience the team as rigid to the point of insensitivity to people. Jesus taught his disciples about the kind of leadership Emmaus calls for—the only kind of leadership Christians are given authority to exercise in Jesus' name.

> Jesus called them to him and said, "You know that the rulers of the Gentiles lord it over them, and their great ones are tyrants over them. It will not be so among you; but whoever wishes to be great among you must be your servant, and whoever wishes to be first among you must be your slave; just as the Son of Man came not to be served but to serve, and to give his life as a ransom for many" (Matthew 20:25-28).

Jesus modeled a leadership style based on the power of love rather than position. Team members and leaders win the pilgrims' respect through spiritual authenticity and willingness to go out of their way for other people's good. Moreover, Lay and Spiritual Directors will model this kind of leadership during team formation if they desire the same from the team on the Walk. Jesus taught the disciples through example more than words and passed on to them the spirit of his gentle style among people. Team leaders do likewise with team members, leading them with love and discipline, affirmation and expectation, while committing to help them give their best on the Walk.

Self-Control

Christians practice self-control by allowing the love of Christ to rule them (see 2 Corinthians 5:14), beginning with the tongue. Team members guard against the temptation to talk rather than listen, to dominate discussions, or to assume the role of a spiritual guru who can tell the pilgrims what they "really need." Team members also avoid the temptation to send coded messages to one another that the pilgrims cannot understand or to make public references to inside jokes that leave the pilgrims feeling like outsiders. James's words are so true: "The tongue is a small member, yet it boasts of great exploits" (Jas. 3:5). Team members avoid letting their team membership become a source or a platform for spiritual pride. Having previously attended an Emmaus event does not imply more maturity in Christ than pilgrims just starting out.

Team members also allow the love of Christ to control their moral and spiritual judgments of the pilgrims. Persons of goodwill and sincere Christian faith differ in their stance (how they discern God's will) on significant moral issues of the day, ranging from drinking and abortion to nuclear weapons and the best ways to care for society's poor. Team members acknowledge this reality and honor other moral positions, even if they disagree with them. They never presume to represent *the* Christian position on difficult issues of the day, and they help pilgrims listen to persons who hold an alternate perspective.

Moreover, team members allow the love of Christ to temper the age-old tendency in religious enthusiasts toward the pharisaic attitudes. Pharisees would require that people's religious lives pass the Pharisees' own spiritual litmus test and conform to their rules for salvation. Pharisees tended to assume that unless people have taken on their particular brand of religious experience or practice, they are not whole. But, not all who attend a Walk need a born-again experience, baptism in the Holy Spirit, commitment to a particular missional concern, special healing, or contemplative prayer experience. Furthermore, the Walk to Emmaus is not the arena in which to promote personal religious experience and emphasis. These "accents" meet needs and may be central to some groups' experiences, but none represents the whole gospel as conveyed by the mainstream of Christian tradition. None alone is necessary for grace, salvation, or a vital Christian life. Team members do the pilgrims and the Emmaus movement a favor by controlling their desire to impose their religious agendas on the Walk, over and above the aims of Emmaus itself.

Pilgrims are at different places on their spiritual journeys and will receive the grace they need on the Walk in different ways. For one person, the Walk is a new and life-altering experience of God's love; for another, the Walk is an enjoyable reinforcement of an already rich faith and practice. For one pilgrim, Emmaus becomes an experience of liberation from an old hurt or hate; for another, it provides an occasion to reorder priorities or commit to a life of service. For still another pilgrim, the Walk is sufficient as a learning experience in Christian theology; for another, it means making some new and close friends. The road to Emmaus begins wherever people are when they are called to participate and ends in the fellowship of friends breaking bread together in communion with the Lord. The only rule of the road is the love of Christ.

TEAM FORMATION

Team formation largely follows a spiritual formation process. Teams don't just happen! A Team Selection Committee that consists of a member of the Emmaus board who serves as committee chair, the Community Spiritual Director, and several members of the Community (non-board members) prayerfully select the team members.

The board selects the Lay and Spiritual Directors for the event; the Lay and Spiritual Directors then participate in the selection committee process. The Team Selection Committee chooses the remainder of the Conference Room Team, which consists of four Assistant Spiritual Directors; three Assistant Lay Directors; one Table Leader and one Assistant Table

Leader for each pilgrim table in the conference room; one to three musicians; and a Board Representative. Emmaus events fall under the authority of the Board of Directors of the local Emmaus Community. The local board comes under the authority of The Upper Room Emmaus Ministries Office, a division of the Discipleship Ministries agency of The United Methodist Church. This relationship provides the continuity from the Emmaus movement through the local Board of Directors to the particular Emmaus event, an essential continuity that maintains the consistency of the Emmaus experience. It also assures that the time, talent, and energies of individual Community members are employed appropriately.

Uniformity in Emmaus events is integral. Communities conduct their Emmaus events according to The Upper Room Emmaus models, which the *Emmaus Ministries Community Manual* explains fully. Leaders use the *Walk to Emmaus Directors' Manual*, which assures consistency in the order of events and the honoring of covenant with The Upper Room. The *Walk to Emmaus Directors' Manual* provides specific directions for the event.

All teams differ. Therefore, although some team members may have experience, the team-formation process includes explanations and discussions of the concept, dynamics, progression of thought, philosophy of, and team behavior on the events. These reminders serve every team well—no matter how many times some members have served on previous teams.

Before agreeing to serve on an Emmaus team, each team member will prayerfully consider the following commitment and willingly accept the level of commitment required.

I understand and accept the commitment and responsibility to attend all Emmaus team meetings for any team on which I agree to serve and to be present throughout the entire Emmaus event (except for emergency or health situations).

Spiritual Formation

Team meetings attempt to establish cohesiveness within the team, a spiritual cohesiveness as the team finds unity in and through Jesus Christ and by the presence of the Holy Spirit at all team meetings. All team members lose their individuality to Jesus and to the team, the body of Christ.

All team members provide parts of one message: the grace of God and the salvation that is ours through Jesus Christ. In all things, let Jesus Christ and other persons come first.

Within the team, without spiritual unity—you in Christ and Christ in you—no unity can exist. With spiritual unity among yourselves and between you and God, you become like one of those who walked to Emmaus. The pilgrims become like the other one who accompanied you, and Jesus Christ will walk with you. Your eyes and those of the pilgrims will be opened, just as the two had their eyes opened after their walk to Emmaus.

The principal goal of team formation is spiritual unity among the team members collectively and individually with God and Jesus Christ under the guidance of the Holy Spirit.

The team's spiritual formation and renewal will model that of the pilgrims' on their event.

Team Conduct

The Emmaus team's mission during the event is to share with the pilgrims the team's vision of faith so that the pilgrims' own perspective on life will change. However, the Emmaus team does not attempt to demonstrate the power of the word during the event nor to stress the need for proclaiming it. Nevertheless, the word is delivered in such a way as to elicit a personal response

Through the team and the Holy Spirit's working through the team, most pilgrims will come to an all-important point in their lives where they can state with meaningful boldness and conviction, "I am a Christian disciple."

Obstacle to Service

Team members need to be free to serve the pilgrims during the weekend without their egos getting in the way.

Egos can become stumbling blocks along the way when team members find themselves calling attention to their own or each other's giftedness or sacrificial goodness or acting out of a personal need for recognition. Egos become stumbling blocks whenever team members make themselves the center of attention with their humor, their presumption of authority, or by displaying their gifts, rather than using their gifts to turn the pilgrims' attention to Jesus Christ and to building the Community.

Egos become stumbling blocks whenever team members talk more than they listen and speak for their table family in the evenings instead of putting the pilgrims forward. Stumbling blocks crop up whenever the pilgrims are led to applaud each speaker after talks, thus calling attention to the person and the needs of the speaker instead of the message the speaker presented; or when team members make a public show of affirming a speaker as he or she leaves the conference room, instead of reserving their accolades for the Prayer Chapel or another time. Whenever speakers make their talks occasions for excessive emotional display or disproportionate amounts of personal witness, thus calling attention primarily to their own experiences and not to the message of their talk, egos have become stumbling blocks.

When team leaders who present general agape overstate how much everyone is sacrificing for the pilgrims, thus making them feel they ought to feel gratitude toward the Emmaus Community rather than letting the agape elicit gratitude and love as a free response, or when persons in support roles allow their personal needs for affirmation or recognition become an issue during an Walk and a point of concern for the team, egos have become stumbling blocks. Egos get in the way when Community members begin to see support functions in the background of the Walk as less important and less desirable avenues of service than visible participation on the Conference Room Team. Those who serve in support roles do represent the invisible backdrop of prayer, sacrificial love, and anonymous servanthood that reflects the Walk's power in the love of God. No one is beyond the need or the privilege of these forms of servanthood, no matter how many times they have served as Lay Director or Spiritual Director or team members.

Practices that highlight distinctions between pilgrims and team members can also become potential instruments of egoism and barriers to Christian community. This barrier arises when teams present any aspects of a Walk or Emmaus itself as a gift from the team to the pilgrims. In this way, the team proudly makes itself the selfless giver of good things and the focus of the pilgrims' gratitude for the weekend. The team's sacrifice always becomes self-evident in time without the team's calling attention to it. Furthermore, Emmaus is not a gift of the team but of the risen Christ who walks with pilgrims and gives them the Holy Spirit through the church and the Emmaus Community. Though the team members have responsibilities as companions who have walked this road before, they are still humble pilgrims on the journey to God and receive grace from the Walk no less than those who are walking to Emmaus for the first time.

Here are some Emmaus team guidelines and procedures that will help the team members indicate their unity with the pilgrims:

- **Team members remain quiet and low-key** about their team status and about their past participation and leadership in Emmaus, for all the reasons stated above. Team members do not keep their identity a secret nor do they attempt to infiltrate the pilgrims with undercover team members. The pilgrims see the entire team on Thursday evening when the Lay Director asks the team to stand in the introductory presentation to Emmaus. Remaining low-key about team identity simply emphasizes their commonality with the pilgrims; they serve humbly and avoid the barrier to community that an attitude of status can present.

- **After the Thursday evening introduction of the team and the Friday morning table assignments**, Assistant Table Leaders serve in anonymity. Few pilgrims remember the persons recognized as team members the previous evening, and it presents no problem if they do. The Assistant Table Leader's role is an exercise in solidarity with the pilgrims, selfless servanthood, and low-key support for the Table Leader and the pilgrims' participation. The persons in this role never make a game of their identity or carry it to the point of deception. Deliberately misleading the pilgrim's plants seeds of suspicion and distrust and works against the purpose of the guideline: development of community on the Walk. Assistant Table Leaders relate to the pilgrims as pilgrims without special status and set an example for wholehearted table participation.

- **Team members are housed in the same facilities** and rooms with the pilgrims, except for the Assistant Lay Directors, Lay Director, Spiritual Director, Music Leaders and Board Representative. Many fruitful conversations occur in the rooms between pilgrims and team members when housed together. No functional reason exists to separate team members from the pilgrims, except for the small inconvenience of returning to the rooms late after the evening team meetings. The only other motives for segregating the team from the pilgrims revolve around privilege and extra convenience that may come from separate quarters, neither of which is congruent with the servant role of the team and the spirit of Emmaus.

- **Team members do not wear their Emmaus crosses or any special Emmaus clothing** that distinguishes them as team members or as veterans of Emmaus until the commissioning,

Closing, and Fourth Day activities. Team members and pilgrims alike begin again and again on the path of Christ. Humility marks the veteran on the spiritual journey—not crosses or clothing that signify the privilege of a few on a Walk.

Emmaus has no place for personal or team glorification. Every part of the method and the manner of Emmaus puts Jesus Christ at the center, calls attention to Christ's goodness and not the team's, and fosters Christian community among all as pilgrims on the Walk.

Discipline

Jesus said, "Follow me" (Matt. 4:9). To paraphrase Dietrich Bonhoeffer in his book *The Cost of Discipleship*, this call is not only to faith but also to obedience. The discipline of the Spirit is hard, and obedience is not an easy matter.

Discipline lies at the heart of an Emmaus team. The discipline of the Spirit makes us servants on a Walk to Emmaus, regardless of the capacity of service. Inasmuch as you accept an invitation to serve on an Emmaus team, do not reluctantly enter the team meeting room through the doorway over which a sign could read, "The Servants' Entrance."

Obedience and Servanthood

1. We serve because Jesus served. We do not serve on an Emmaus team to have a great time for ourselves, although the experience enriches and blesses the team members. We will receive some gifts from Jesus Christ. He does that as we serve; however, *we are here to serve the pilgrims.*

2. We serve on a team with a willingness to take direction from the Lay Director, Assistant Lay Directors, and the Spiritual Director. If you have a problem with authority and cannot submit to direction, then say no when asked to serve on a team. Discipline underlies the character of the Emmaus team, its formation and life. Without such discipline, the weekend becomes vulnerable to chaos.

3. We are servants who submit to the Holy Spirit. *No team member, including clergy, will be singled out individually for any special recognition.* We are *one* team, *one* message, *one* body of Christ. Only God is to be glorified on an Emmaus event.

The main objective is not for the pilgrims to have a joyful encounter with the team, but rather for the team to be the *servant-instrument* subordinate to the Holy Spirit so the Holy Spirit can direct the pilgrims into a joyful encounter with Jesus Christ.

The Walk's procedures and mechanics, although vital to its success, are of secondary importance to its spiritual dimension. The *Walk to Emmaus Directors' Manual* spells out the procedures: the activity, the time, the supplies needed, etc. Team members review all these aspects at team meetings and fix them firmly in their minds. But if some detail is overlooked on the event itself, the Holy Spirit will have a hand on the situation; there is no cause for alarm. The key: remain flexible.

TEAM MEETINGS

Team meetings provide the process through which a group of individuals becomes a team. The objectives are spiritual and functional unity—one body in unity with the Lord and with one another. Prior to the first team meeting, a board member who is not on the team for the upcoming set of walks conducts an orientation session. The *Walk to Emmaus Directors' Manual* describes this orientation session.

The following information briefly summarizes what happens at team meetings. Appendix A includes more detailed information.

1. Team formation includes twenty-three to twenty-six hours together in order to accomplish the needed tasks. This time is in addition to the orientation session.

2. Team meetings begin with a brief meditation followed by Communion.

3. After Communion, a brief "floating" accountability group convenes.

4. The Lay Director selects a prayer partner for each team member.

5. For each talk preview, the speaker will come with his or her talk completed and timed, and with final visual aids (props, posters, and/or electronic media). Prior to each preview, the prayer partner will pray for the speaker, the message of the talk, and the team response to the talk.

6. Following the talk presentation, the team forms table groups to discuss the talk, which serves as a critique experience. Those who will serve as table leaders on the Walk lead the discussions. Appendix C furnishes a critique sheet for talk previews. This discussion and critique process achieve the following:

   a) allows practice in being a Table Leader and leading discussion;

   b) provides a preview of the talk and an opportunity to focus on important elements of the talk; and

   c) helps the team members develop their talks in rhythm and continuity with the others.

   After the discussion, the speaker returns to the room and each of the Table Leaders offers a critique of the presentation, reflecting upon points raised in the table discussion. Team members critique the talk against the major points in the talk outline and the suitability of personal witness remarks. The "Table Dynamics" section of this manual summarizes the key points of each talk.

   Although individuals take responsibility for the talks, the talks also reflect the collective wisdom and spirit of the team critique. There are no lone rangers on Emmaus events.

   When a team member presents his or her talk and receives the team's comments, the talk no longer belongs to the speaker alone but to the entire team. A speaker should not surprise the team on the weekend with a radically different talk than the one previewed without consulting the Lay and/or Spiritual Director for permission and guidance.

7. An orderly sequence exists in the development of thought processes and dynamics throughout the talks. Be aware of how each talk fits with the talks that precede and follow

it. The entire team, not just the speakers, maintains a consciousness of the dynamics and processes of the event.

8. The "Overview of the Event" section details the sequence and experiences of the Walk to Emmaus. Its success hinges on the team's embracing the orderly aspect of the entire event in both practice and spirit.

9. Maintaining the building blocks of the Walk's talks is vital. Speakers aim to make talk sequentially valid each day and in concert with the related talks on the other days.

10. In addition to the *daily* sequence of the talks, another sequence leads across the walk. Therefore, the processes of the event provide not just a line of thought, but rather a web of thought.

Flow of Lay Talks across the Three Days*

1st Day	PRIORITY	PRIESTHOOD OF ALL BELIEVERS	LIFE OF PIETY
2nd Day	GROW THROUGH STUDY	CHRISTIAN ACTION	DISCIPLESHIP
3rd Day	CHANGING OUR WORLD	BODY OF CHRIST	FOURTH DAY
	The process of using our mind; deciding what to study, what to change.	To set a priority for our ministry; the ways a Christian serves.	Summary talks on living the life of grace.

*The PERSEVERANCE Talk is a lay talk presented on Day Three after the BODY OF CHRIST talk and before the FOURTH DAY talk.

SECTION 4— OVERVIEW OF THE WALK

Emmaus leaders generally know much more about *what* to do and *how* to do it than *why* we do what we do the way we do it. This overview gives commentary not only on the *what* and *how* of the event procedures but also on the *why* of the Emmaus structure. Understanding Emmaus on this level guards against unwarranted or arbitrary alterations in the Emmaus model. Every piece has its meaningful place in the event's architecture, both structurally and theologically. When leaders lead from an understanding of the model, it enhances team formation, leadership training, and the Emmaus events.

What follows is a day-by-day overview of the Walk to Emmaus event. After summarizing each day's activities, the overview explores some parts of that day's schedule in more detail with regard to procedure and purpose. A section titled "General Remarks" then addresses some critical aspects of the walk as a whole. A chart of the three-day overview is included at the end of this section and has proven to be a helpful handout for training of Emmaus teams and leaders.

A TRINITARIAN FRAMEWORK

The three days of a Walk to Emmaus event have distinct phases. The focus of Day One is *God and the grace God offers*. We may view the aim of Day One as opening our *minds* to the need for a vital relationship with God, thus ending with LIFE OF PIETY.

The focus of Day Two is *Jesus Christ and our life as a response to grace*. We may view the aim of Day Two as moving our *hearts* to greater commitment to live in union with Jesus Christ, thus ending with DISCIPLESHIP.

The focus of Day Three is the *Holy Spirit and the pilgrims' call* to be part of the Christian community in action. We may view the aim of Day Three as encouraging the *body* of Christ to take action in the world in the power of the Holy Spirit, thus ending with FOURTH DAY.

Thursday Night

Thursday evening has three distinct components. The first, Send-Off, involves the Community and the new pilgrims. The second is for the Conference Room Team and pilgrims. The third is for the Community (Sponsors' Hour). The pilgrims arrive, register, and have a brief time of fellowship with the Community whose members receive the pilgrims in a spirit of hospitality.

The Community serves as host, and the pilgrims are the guests. The Lay Director leads the Community and pilgrims in the Send-Off, which concludes with the pilgrims and Conference Room Team going to the conference room. After Send-Off, the Community gathers in the chapel for Sponsors' Hour and then departs the facility.

Send-Off

When all pilgrims are present, the Lay Director calls out the names of the weekend pilgrims, making no distinctions between pilgrims and team members. The Lay Director asks them to repeat their names aloud when they hear their names called to join the lineup of those attending the Walk. The Lay Director calls the individuals by name and asks them to repeat their name for two reasons: to be certain of the correct pronunciation and to provide an opportunity for each one to speak in front of a large group. This speaking aloud before the group helps develop future leaders. When all the pilgrims have joined the line, the Community demonstrates its support of them in some respectful way, such as applause, rather than hoots or whistles. The point is to affirm and encourage pilgrims rather than frighten them or make them feel uncomfortable. As they are led to the conference room or retreat center, the Community serenades them with a lively song.

Sponsors' Hour

After the Send-Off, once the pilgrims have left the assembly room to begin their event, the sponsors and others present gather in the chapel for a time of prayer for the pilgrims and their three-day experience. For Chrysalis, if the Parents' Meeting is to follow the Sponsors' Hour, the parents of the pilgrims will take part in the Sponsors' Hour as well. The Community Spiritual Director or a board member leads Sponsors' Hour or arranges for someone in the Community to lead it.

This brief service consists of prayer for each of the pilgrims by name. The leader may read aloud the name of each pilgrim. As a name is read, his or her sponsor walks to the front where the pilgrims' crosses are draped across the altar. The sponsor takes a cross for his or her pilgrim and hangs it across the arm of a large standing cross. The individual crosses will remain there throughout the three days as a symbolic focus of prayer in the Prayer Chapel. Those gathered pray silently for each pilgrim as his or her cross is carried forward. If a sponsor is not present and did not arrange for a proxy, any Community member may spontaneously stand in for the sponsor and carry the cross forward.

Thursday Night's Aim

In the conference room, the pilgrims gather to meet the others with whom they will journey; to hear a description of what lies before them; and, in a time of spiritual retreat, to prepare themselves inwardly for the event, which formally begins the following morning. After the Thursday night video, the Spiritual Director encourages the pilgrims' awareness of where they are on their spiritual pilgrimages and reminds them to keep the silence for this one night. Following night prayer, the pilgrims retire to their rooms or remain in the chapel for prayer if they choose. The end of the period of preparation and silence coincides the next morning with a service of Holy Communion and the beginning of the three-day journey.

Thursday night's agenda is intended to allay the pilgrims' fears, awaken interest, and invite them to be serious about profiting from the three days to come. This evening is their first direct contact with team members who want to win their confidence by being friendly, natural, and positive. The team sets a good example for the pilgrims by being themselves and establishing a positive tone.

Thursday Night Video

Emmaus Ministries recommends the Thursday night video for several reasons. The visual medium of the video helps each event get off to a solid, dependable, and nonthreatening start, while removing team members from the spotlight of performance. Above all, the Thursday night video invites the pilgrims to reflect honestly on their own responses to Jesus.

Spiritual Director's Meditation

The meditation invites the pilgrims to realize the potential value of these three days apart, to locate themselves on their own spiritual journeys, and to reflect upon the place of God in their lives. The Spiritual Director's comments provide a focus for their thoughts and meditations during the silence.

Thursday Evening Team Meeting

Thursday night's brief team meeting respects the call to silence and returns everyone to the sleeping quarters as quickly as possible. One agenda item of the meeting is to finalize the table assignments for Friday morning. If possible, seat pilgrims who are close friends or members of the same church at different tables. Assignments for each table would include a variety of ages, ethnicities, churches, and denominations. Each table arrangement will provide room for making new friends and space between old friends who may inhibit each other's sharing. The Lay Director shares preliminary table assignments so the team members can alert the Lay Director to any necessary changes.

At this meeting, the Lay or Spiritual Director also reviews Friday's flow briefly, naming those team members who will be giving talks. The speakers are told how they will be reminded when their time comes to get dressed and go to the Prayer Chapel in preparation for their talk. The team meeting ends with a time of prayer, which would include special mention of the next day's speakers.

Friday, the First Day

Friday Morning Communion

On Friday morning, we begin our spiritual journey with the nourishment of the bread of life in Holy Communion. In the spirit of the evening silence and of the first day, the Spiritual Director conducts this service in a simple, straightforward manner using the liturgy in the worshipbook but without singing or passing the peace. The rule of silence does not mean the Spiritual Director conducts the Communion service without spoken liturgy. The silence simply serves to curb casual conversation so persons can listen to God during the late evening and early morning hours. On Friday morning, the first and only words heard are words within the word—the liturgy, scripture, and actions of worship that direct our attention to God.

The Spiritual Director's "sermon" will briefly reiterate a word of life from the scripture that relates to the theme of the day: Ephesians 2:8-10. Or, the reading of a scripture alone can suffice in anticipation of "The Loving Father (Prodigal Son)" meditation that follows immediately upon Holy Communion. A lengthy message (more than five minutes), no matter how well done, would be inappropriate. In some cases, Spiritual Directors prefer simply to present the "The Loving Father (Prodigal Son)" meditation at the time of the sermon during the Communion service.

The "The Loving Father (Prodigal Son)" meditation sets the theme for the day: God's unconditional love and offer of a personal relationship no matter who we are or what our condition. The meditation invites us to come to our senses, to open ourselves to God's welcoming love, and to begin the return home to live our life with God in grace.

PRIORITY

The PRIORITY talk is part one of the fifteen-part short course in Christianity. The speaker highlights the importance of priorities in human life and creates an openness to evaluating priorities. This talk appeals to persons based on their reason and experience, not based on their faith. This approach draws the pilgrims into the universal question of what is worth living for in this life and sets the stage for the Christian answer to be heard later as the event unfolds. For this reason, the speaker presents this talk without religious presumption or God language, such as, "God ought to be every true Christian's priority" or "When I met Jesus, my priorities changed." Such messages rush the event, can bring closure to the question of priorities prematurely, and can inhibit honest discussion. This first talk of the weekend sets a positive, objective, open-minded, and accepting tone. An Assistant Lay Director who is an experienced speaker gives the first talk to get the event off to a good start. This practice keeps a Table Leader at the table during the first discussion period of the weekend.

Atmosphere: The pilgrims may begin to sense a desire for something more and may experience a spiritual awakening at this point. Previous chapel meditations have brought the pilgrims face-to-face with Jesus Christ. In general, they may feel tense, but they have been stirred to consider their priorities in light of their commitment to Christ.

PREVENIENT GRACE

The talk on PRIORITY reminds us that as human beings we can rise above instinct and set priorities that will give our lives meaning and direction. The PREVENIENT GRACE talk tells us that irrespective of our human priorities, God's priority comes in loving us; God has loved us before our conception, and God reaches out to us again and again with the offer of a saving relationship.

Atmosphere: The pilgrims may still feel at a loss to know what they have gotten themselves into by attending this Walk to Emmaus. This second talk helps them focus their attention on God's grace. With this talk, they start realizing that they hunger for God's grace in their life.

PRIESTHOOD OF ALL BELIEVERS

The PRIESTHOOD OF ALL BELIEVERS talk challenges all of us—both lay and clergy—to serve as representatives of God's grace by reaching out to people with words and deeds of God's unconditional love.

Atmosphere: The atmosphere of the weekend remains one of the mind rather than the heart. Most pilgrims will participate; others will still hold back.

JUSTIFYING GRACE

The JUSTIFYING GRACE talk invites us to accept God's love and God's gracious offer of a relationship, which gives us new life through Jesus Christ.

The introduction of general agape at the end of the JUSTIFYING GRACE talk illustrates and begins to make real the grace the speakers have talked about throughout the day—an abundant love that precedes any response on our part but wants to win our hearts.

Atmosphere: The reading of agape letters from other Emmaus and Cursillo Communities has a great impact on the pilgrims at this point. This can be an emotional time for them; other people care about them and are sacrificing and praying for them. A new understanding of the reality of Christian community, its love and support, is awakened. This revelation may openly overwhelm many pilgrims.

LIFE OF PIETY

The LIFE OF PIETY talk describes and begins to make real the lifestyle of a person who has accepted God's love in Jesus Christ and who makes living in the grace of that relationship life's priority—a person who has given his or her heart to God. The Emmaus Road prayer experience provides an opportunity to begin to do what the LIFE OF PIETY talk expresses—to enter into personal relationship with God through prayerful dialogue with Jesus Christ.

Atmosphere: The pilgrims still may have lingering doubts and yet have a growing desire to be a more devoted member of Christ's church.

The sharing of talk summaries and posters, skits, poems, and songs is a fun time for creatively recapping the day through each table's insights and images of the five talks. As the day ends during night prayer in the chapel, the Spiritual Director reviews the message of the day and assures the pilgrims that no pat responses are expected, only honesty with themselves and one another and giving themselves wholeheartedly to the Walks pilgrimage in the presence of the Lord.

Meal Graces, "De Colores," and Joke Time

The first day gradually introduces the pilgrims to many new people, procedures, and songs that become significant parts of their life together for three days. Breakfast on the first day begins with a prayer by the Lay Director who then explains the talk and table process. Before lunch, the Music Director teaches the Emmaus meal graces and "De Colores." The Music Director will also explain the Benedictine tradition behind praying before and after meals and tell the tradition about "De Colores." This explanation gives meaning to these practices and songs for the Walk. The pilgrims begin to discover that on the Emmaus event they participate in there is a deep and vital spiritual tradition. The Music Director's Checklist in the *Walk to Emmaus Directors' Manual* and the book *Music Directors* provides these explanations.

At lunchtime or suppertime, an Assistant Lay Director introduces joke time as an Emmaus tradition. The joke time introduction relays three primary rules: (1) jokes are brief; (2) jokes are clean; and (3) jokes are funny. After the pilgrims have begun their meal, an Assistant leads off with a joke. The Assistant Lay Director then provides leadership for joke time by calling on others who want to share a joke or story. The Assistant Lay Director concludes joke time, and the Music Director leads the group in singing the meal benediction.

The introduction of the jokes provides some comic relief toward the end of a heavy day and becomes a fun way for the pilgrims to get to know one another as human beings. Joke time is part of the leadership development process. It affords opportunities for people to stand in front of a group and speak. Joke time also reminds everybody that Christians can laugh and have a good time. Keep in mind that the jokes need to remain clean and fun for everyone and not work against the Walk's purpose by becoming offensive or prejudicial. The Assistant Lay Directors will remind the group of the three rules and cut off joke time if necessary. If persons—especially team members—feel unsure about the appropriateness of their jokes, they probably should not tell them. Joke time becomes a part of each mealtime hereafter as the schedule permits.

Introducing General Agape

The speaker introduces agape in the closing portion of the talk on JUSTIFYING GRACE. To illustrate the agape love undergirding the pilgrims on the event, the speaker shares a few of the many general agape letters or banners from other Emmaus communities and explains the 72-Hour Prayer Vigil. The Assistant Lay Directors post the general agape as the speaker shares the letters. If for some reason, the JUSTIFYING GRACE speaker cannot explain agape as part of the talk, the Spiritual Director introduces agape after the talk and before the table discussions. With the introduction of general agape on Friday afternoon, the pilgrims encounter again the message of God's prevenient and justifying grace: Though they were not aware of it until now, God's love has surrounded them through the prayers and sacrifices of caring people since the event began.

Team members continue to share general agape letters from other Communities and table agape throughout the event. On Friday the walls of the conference room are blank for most of the day; but over the course of the three days, the walls gradually fill with colorful reminders of the sacrifices of countless people who are holding the pilgrims in their prayers. Table agape first appears at the supper table Friday evening. The pilgrims will receive individual agape letters from family and friends only on Sunday afternoon after the FOURTH DAY talk. These letters enrich the message of going forth to be the love of Christ for others and prepare the pilgrims to embrace the world that they reenter with the love they have received.

Friday Evening Team Meeting

The team meeting is not a time to gossip or to violate the pilgrims' confidences, nor is it a time for group analysis of pilgrims. The aim is to celebrate the day and help team members deal with difficulties that might detract from the rest of the event for a pilgrim, a table, or the entire group. Table Leaders who struggle with how to respond to pilgrims' personal problems will talk with the Spiritual Director, not the entire team.

The agenda for Friday evening's team meeting includes a review of the day's dynamics and a checkup on each table family. The Lay or Spiritual Director begins the meeting by asking team members to share their celebrations from the day; then the leader can request sharing of concerns. This order helps everyone focus on God's presence first and on problems second. During the meeting, each Table Leader receives a chance to report on the health of his or her table family and their interactions. Table Leaders can benefit from the counsel of the whole team on how to deal with resistance at the tables or difficulties with persons, but should first seek counsel of the Spiritual Director. The team meeting is the only time the Lay or Spiritual Director gives direction to the whole team with words of affirmation as well as correction.

This being the last team meeting, the leader briefly reviews the schedule and assignments for Saturday as well as Sunday, along with expectations of the team members about their participation. The meeting closes with prayer, which includes praying for the remaining speakers.

Saturday, the Second Day

Saturday begins with morning prayer in the chapel. The Spiritual Director's meditation on "Four Responses to Christ," which describes the responses of four persons in the Gospels to Jesus, sets the theme for the day with the repeated questions: Is this your response? What is your response to Jesus?

GROW THROUGH STUDY

The talk on GROW THROUGH STUDY calls us to enlarge our understanding of God and God's hurting world by giving our minds to Christ. This talk builds on the LIFE OF PIETY talk's description of the lifestyle of the person whose priority is living in grace.

Atmosphere: The pilgrims are experiencing mixed feelings. All are experiencing the pull of God. The pilgrim stands at a crossroads. *Can I be like this? Do I want this? Where will this lead?*

MEANS OF GRACE

The MEANS OF GRACE talk presents the sacred moments by which we celebrate and open ourselves regularly to God's redeeming grace as people and as the church. It helps to have blank three-by-five cards on each table on which pilgrims may pose questions about this talk. The Dying Moments Communion service follows this talk immediately. Pilgrims receive the opportunity to respond to Christ's healing grace by giving up a nagging sin or wound in their lives and opening to the new life God grants them in Christ.

Following lunch and a long break, the Spiritual Director takes a few minutes to respond to the written questions about MEANS OF GRACE. The Spiritual Director then invites tables to begin making visits to the chapel for group prayer, another opportunity to respond to grace, to share our life in Christ, and to experience God's love with one another.

Atmosphere: Thoughts and concepts start to come together. The pilgrims have grown in their trust of the experience, of the persons at their tables, and of the love of God for them. Now they begin to trust enough to share honestly how they feel and how God has moved in their lives. Be ready to help them share these feelings.

CHRISTIAN ACTION

The talk on CHRISTIAN ACTION calls us to give our hands and feet to Christ, bearing witness to Christ's friendship and love in all we say and do. This talk completes the three-part description (piety, study, and action) of the lifestyle of the person who chooses living in grace as a life priority.

Atmosphere: After lunch on Saturday, the pilgrims may feel emotionally drained. Most will have accepted the call to a new or renewed life in Christ and will eagerly embrace the opportunity to learn more about "how."

OBSTACLES TO GRACE

The OBSTACLES TO GRACE talk explores the obstacles of sin that we encounter as we set out to live in grace and the ways we overcome these obstacles.

Atmosphere: At this point, the pilgrims may wonder why they have not realized God's great love before. Their openness to the message of this talk will help them understand that sin is the obstacle to God's grace.

The Saturday evening meal offers an oasis of refreshment toward the end of a rich though draining day, featuring dinner by candlelight and entertainment.

DISCIPLESHIP

The talk on DISCIPLESHIP summarizes and focuses the message of the event thus far: persons who accept God's hand of friendship and seek above all to live in the grace of Jesus Christ through the disciplines of piety, study, and action are true disciples of Jesus. Moreover, the lifestyle of an authentic disciple who lives his or her whole life in relationship with Jesus Christ reflects the qualities of Jesus' own life and ministry.

Atmosphere: Pilgrims will experience new feelings of expectation and joy. Chapel visits have been completed. Pilgrims are thinking about all they left behind and the difficulties they will face. *Can I really change the world?*

Once again, the zestful sharing of talk summaries and posters by tables reviews the message of the day.

Night prayer takes the form of the Candlelight service in which the Emmaus Community, having already prayed for each pilgrim in a preceding service of Holy Communion, gathers in the sanctuary pews of the sanctuary and surrounds the pilgrims with the light of Christ to move them closer to a realization of the sheer grace of God's love. When the Community has withdrawn, the pilgrims enter into a time of prayer and recommitment in which they receive another opportunity to respond to the grace of Jesus Christ, who now calls them to follow and to rededicate themselves as his disciples. After informal refreshments and fellowship, the pilgrims go to bed. Usually, the leaders hold no team meeting that night.

Dying Moments and Holy Communion Service

"Dying moments" refer to specific sins, guilt, wounds, disappointments, burdens, or brokenness that we experience as living death in our lives. Some Spiritual Directors develop the MEANS OF GRACE talk around this theme, defining each "sacred moment" as a means by which God overcomes some form of living death at work in us and restores us to life. The Dying Moments Communion service then flows naturally out of the MEANS OF GRACE talk. Other Spiritual Directors who do not present the MEANS OF GRACE talk through the image of dying moments develop the theme effectively during an introduction and a meditation in the Dying Moments Communion service

How is the Dying Moments Communion service carried out? The Spiritual Director explains and personally illustrates dying moments in a Communion meditation and invites the pilgrims to get in touch with a part of their lives that needs to die or be released to make space for new life. In following an abbreviated order of service outlined in the *Walk to Emmaus 3-Day Schedule* and beginning on page 26 of the *Worship Booklet for Pilgrims*, the Spiritual Director invites the pilgrims to break off a piece of bread as a sign of their own brokenness as they name aloud their dying moment.

The Spiritual Director goes first, breaking off a piece of the loaf and placing it in the empty basket (located on the Communion table and, when possible, at the foot of a cross) while naming aloud his or her dying moment, using a word or short phrase. The Spiritual Director then invites the pilgrims to come forward to do likewise and return to their seats. At this point, the Spiritual Director returns to his or her seat. Two or three team members go forward first to model how to name briefly a dying moment.

After everyone has participated and is seated, the Spiritual Director lifts the basket before the group and continues with the Words of Pardon as printed in the *Walk to Emmaus 3-Day Schedule*. The basket is then placed at the foot of the cross, and the Spiritual Director uncovers the second loaf and the cup and invites the group to join in The Great Thanksgiving as printed in the *Worship Booklet for Pilgrims* beginning on page 29.

After the consecration of the elements, the Spiritual Director then invites the pilgrims to come forward a second time to receive the Communion elements by intinction (dipping the piece of bread into the cup of juice). When all have partaken, they share in expressing the Resurrection joy of the moment through the Prayer after Receiving (page 34, *Worship Booklet for Pilgrims*), words of instruction by the Spiritual Director, a well-chosen closing song, and a benediction. The Lay Director will then dismiss the group for lunch.

The Spiritual Director plans the Dying Moments Communion service ahead of time, including the arrangement of the Communion table with the first loaf of bread, the empty basket, and the cross; the Communion elements of a second loaf and the juice; the scripture and meditation; whether the Dying Moments time will be in silence or have quiet background instrumental music; the closing song led by the Music Director; and instructions for the best flow to and from the Communion table. Several Assistant Lay Directors who sit at the front of the chapel can be first in line to break the bread and name their dying moment, setting an example for the pilgrims. When the seating arrangement allows, pilgrims are asked to sit in the chapel by table groups to foster the development of Christian community at the tables. The *Walk to Emmaus 3-Day Schedule* offers complete explanations and directions. Clear instructions will engage the pilgrims' full participation.

Questions about Dying Moments

Why must pilgrims name their dying moments aloud? Healing power resides in the public act of an honest confession of sin, need, or faith. When Jesus healed the man with the withered hand in the synagogue, he asked him to "come forward" and to "stretch out your hand" (Mark 3:1-6). The public act requires us to admit our humanness and our need for grace, which are no secret to anyone except ourselves. Using symbolic words or short phrases such as *fear, disappointment in myself,* or *April 15th* frees each pilgrim to participate honestly without feeling pressured or embarrassed to reveal personal details. The value of naming our dying moments aloud is not in other people's hearing what we say but in the outward act of admitting our need and giving our brokenness to God in the presence of others. Sharing aloud in the sanctity of the cloistered environment is another step in the process of building community.

What is distinctive about this ritual? The Dying Moments Communion service represents visually the healing and forgiving grace of God. We take part in the new covenant offered in Christ and practice the means of grace known as Holy Communion. Just as Jesus used the broken bread to represent his broken body, the Spiritual Director invites the pilgrims to break a piece of bread from a loaf and to name some aspect of their own brokenness. The words of confession, both communally in the prayer and individually in the naming of dying moments, are symbolically laid at the foot of the cross and the words of pardon are offered and received. Then the Spiritual Director speaks the words of consecration over the second loaf of bread and the cup of juice. The pilgrims can understand that though we may be broken by the sin and pain in our lives, Christ's body was broken and his blood was shed so we may receive healing, forgiveness, and wholeness.

Lunch and Break Following Dying Moments Communion

For some pilgrims, the lunchtime following Dying Moments Communion may be a time of reflection—the early phases of processing and evaluating what transpired during Dying Moments Communion. The Assistant Lay Directors, with guidance from the Spiritual Director, will consider the suitability of joke time following this meal. Having jokes so soon after the highly emotional and spiritual experience may be an inappropriate intrusion into the solemnity and sacredness of the Dying Moments Communion.

The schedule indicates a long break following this lunch period, the longest break of the weekend; the leaders need to preserve this time. This break is not the place to make up lost time in the schedule. The pilgrims have come through an emotional and spiritually deepening event. They need this long break to process all that has developed.

Discussion on MEANS OF GRACE

To facilitate the question-and-answer period following Dying Moments Communion and lunch, the Spiritual Director can respond to the pilgrims' questions written ahead of time on three-by-five cards. This approach allows the Spiritual Director to review the questions during the break with other clergy and select the questions he or she can respond to best and briefly. The Spiritual Director then explains that time does not permit answering all the questions, but that he/she and the Assistant Spiritual Directors will be available informally at other times to answer additional questions. This approach means the Assistant Lay Directors must distribute three-by-five cards to the tables *before* the MEANS OF GRACE talk. Early in the talk, the Spiritual Director encourages pilgrims to write their questions on the cards. The Assistant Lay Directors collect the cards afterward and give them to the Spiritual Director for review.

The MEANS OF GRACE talk emphasizes what Christians basically agree upon about the means of grace and the human needs they meet, especially in more ecumenical settings. The discussion period will deal with questions for clarification and the fostering of appreciation for our common ground as Christians, not to highlight our differences. This is not a time for theological debate and argument over the beliefs of different denominations represented in the room, which inevitably stir up feelings of contention and discontent. If necessary, remind pilgrims that gifts come through differences of belief among denominations and that tolerance is a Christian virtue. Emmaus does not promote uniformity of belief but unity in the Spirit among members of the Christian community.

In the fifteen minutes provided, Spiritual Directors will exercise their own judgment in answering questions and will encourage persons to take their unanswered questions back to their pastors and learn more about their own church beliefs.

Chapel Visits by Tables

The pilgrims journey through several levels of community during the event. Having come to the event out of the wider Christian community, they become aware of an Emmaus Community that supports them with acts of agape, sacrifice, and prayer. They are part of a Community that has been forming among the pilgrims and team. In addition, they share the most intimate level of community with those at their tables. At this time, the pilgrims receive an opportunity to give expression to the closest and most intimate experience of spiritual community on the event by going to the chapel with their tables for prayer. This time of prayer involves *only* the table group. This prayer experience develops the community-building process for the table group and offers a time for sharing in trust and in confidence.

The *Walk to Emmaus 3-Day Schedule* gives helpful instructions about table groups praying together in the chapel. The method of passing the cross from one person to the next as a way of taking turns in prayer encourages each person's participation but allows each the freedom to pray aloud or silently. It is crucial to support the individual who decides to pray silently. To evidence this support, the Assistant Table Leader prays last. If one or more pilgrims have prayed silently, the Assistant Table Leader will then pray silently. The Table Leader begins and ends this prayer experience. The Table Leader should not try to create a great prayer experience or fill in periods of silence with verbal prayer. This time of prayer can be a simple sharing of feelings before God without concern about what to say. The Table Leader sets the tone with humble and honest prayer, making sure no one feels pressured to pray. On the way to the chapel, the Table Leader reminds the group members of the Spiritual Director's request that they take no more than fifteen minutes and then help the group honor that time frame.

Table Leaders alert the Assistant Lay Directors to their table members' readiness to go to the chapel so the directors can schedule and coordinate the chapel visits. By coordinating the visits, the Assistant Lay Directors make it possible for all the tables to visit the chapel during the available breaks and table discussion times. This will prevent two or three groups from going to the chapel at the same time or one group interrupting another group already using the space. The Assistant Lay Directors can also direct table groups to additional sites prepared for table group prayer.

Saturday Evening Dinner and Entertainment

Table and dining room decorations, a more elaborate meal and service, and after-dinner entertainment create a festive atmosphere for Saturday night dinner. There is no joke time after this meal. This time is received as an act of agape, an experience of being given a party unexpectedly and treated like God's special children for whom no amount of care is too much. Entertainment consists of fifteen to twenty minutes of music, drama, or humorous skits prepared by members of the Emmaus Community or kitchen crew. Most communities have no trouble making the Saturday evening special.

Teams keep Saturday dinner plans in perspective, because more is yet to come. Spending excessive amounts of time and energy preparing the special meal, decorations, and entertainment can delay the evening schedule. The agape message of the pilgrims' worth can be reinforced through simple means.

Candlelight

Candlelight moves the pilgrims to a deeper realization of God's love and demonstrates the support of a Christian community for their life as faithful followers of Jesus Christ. Candlelight, while a moving experience both for pilgrims and Community, does not attempt to create a mountaintop experience for its own sake. Candlelight prepares the way for the time of personal prayer and recommitment that follows upon the Emmaus Community's departure. In the Gospels, many people sought Jesus for the grace of healing and forgiveness, but fewer heeded the call to follow as Jesus journeyed toward the cross. Dying Moments Communion gives the pilgrims an opportunity to bring their needs to Jesus, but Candlelight encourages them to take the next step of rededication as disciples in their response to God's grace. For this reason, Candlelight and the time of prayer that follows complete the unfolding of Saturday's theme of response to the grace of Jesus Christ.

At least an hour prior to the Candlelight service, while the pilgrims share summaries and representations in the conference room, the Emmaus Community gathers quietly in the chapel to celebrate Holy Communion and to pray for each of the pilgrims by name. Someone in the Community takes responsibility for this event. This person plans for clergy and music leadership for the pre-Candlelight gathering and Communion and makes sure Communion bulletins and candle supplies are ready. The brief Communion meditation addresses the situation of Candlelight and the Community's presence or a Fourth Day witness speaks to the continuing walk with God. This is not time or the place for a clergyperson to rehearse Sunday's sermon.

Following the Communion service, "Jesus, Jesus" is rehearsed, candles distributed, and the Community reminded of the Candlelight procedures. The Assistant Lay Directors alert the Community to the pilgrims' approach. With the lights in the chapel turned out and all candles lit, the Community sings the prayer song "Jesus, Jesus" in a round repeatedly as the pilgrims enter the chapel.

"Jesus, Jesus, can I tell you how I feel,
You have given me your Spirit,
I love you so."

This prayer song is the only song used at Candlelight and the only verse to be sung.

Community members preserve the integrity of the service and do not block or confuse the pilgrims' entry by reaching out to touch them as they pass. Community members reaching out to touch the pilgrims can obscure the vision pilgrims often have of God's love filling the sanctuary, seeing Jesus in the faces of the people, and the presence of a heavenly host with the communion of saints. Remember the weekend is for the pilgrims; let them have their own experience. Leaders encourage family members or friends from far away to sit on the center aisle or on the front pews facing the chancel area so the pilgrims for whom they have come can see them.

The pilgrims pass through the candlelit Community and gather in the chancel area facing the Community. When the Community stops singing, the Spiritual Director uses the narrative provided in the *Walk to Emmaus 3-Day Schedule* to explain what is happening. The Spiritual Director then asks the pilgrims to sing "Jesus, Jesus" in response as an expression of gratitude. Having learned "Jesus, Jesus" earlier in the day and with the support of the team and the Music Director, the pilgrims sing "Jesus, Jesus" as a round. After the pilgrims have sung two rounds, the community begins to slowly file out, moving forward past the pilgrims with candles lit, then out of the sanctuary, starting from the back pews. Upon exiting the chapel, the Community members extinguish their candles, go to their cars, and depart quietly.

Prayer Following Candlelight

When the Community has departed, the Music Director draws the pilgrims' singing to a close and the Spiritual Director addresses them with an explanation of the period of prayer that follows. The Spiritual Director states clearly and specifically the purpose of the time in the chapel—prayer and recommitment, the different ways in which they can use this time, and how they will recognize the prayer time's conclusion. Pilgrims may pray alone in their seats, alone at the altar, with the Spiritual Director or an Assistant Spiritual Director at the altar, with a friend, or speak with the Spiritual Director or an Assistant Spiritual Director in a designated area. Suggest that a nonverbal sign (hands turned upward at the altar rail) indicates a pilgrim's desire for prayer with one of the Spiritual Directors. The pilgrims may use this chapel time to express themselves in prayer in whatever manner they choose in response to the impulse of God's love in their hearts. Pilgrims reach out when they are ready; they, not team members, initiate the reaching out. With specific instructions, the pilgrims know what is expected and what is possible, which frees them to use the time to their benefit with minimum inhibitions.

All five Spiritual Directors are present for this service, two at or near the altar for prayer with pilgrims and the others available for spiritual counsel in a secondary area. Team members bear in mind that the event is for the pilgrims and avoid tying up the Spiritual Directors for their own needs. Team members have the period of team formation, as well as other times during the event, to meet with the Spiritual Directors.

When the Walk Spiritual Director senses that the pilgrims have made the most of the time, the service usually concludes with a prayer by the Spiritual Director and/or a meditative solo. The leader reminds the pilgrims that they may remain in the chapel, but informal refreshments await them and they are free to go to bed when they choose. The Spiritual Director remains in the chapel for those who wish to stay.

While some people may become emotional during their time of personal prayer, the service is not designed to evoke emotional response. There is no mood-setting background music or evangelistic appeal. After the Spiritual Director explains the service and gives the invitation to prayer and recommitment, the leading of the Holy Spirit in people's hearts provides the only leadership. For thirty minutes or so, the pilgrims remain in the dimly lit chapel to respond to God's love and renew their commitment to Christ. Spiritual Directors make themselves available to pilgrims but do not prompt them for conversation or commitments.

Each post-Candlelight prayer time is unique and serves the needs of the pilgrims in its own way. On some Emmaus events, many pilgrims will desire prayer and counsel with Spiritual Directors or seek out the spiritual support of one another. On other events, solitary prayer characterizes the prayer time and few, if any, seek out the Spiritual Directors. The level of visible activity does not serve as a barometer of the value or success of the evening.

Sunday, the Third Day

Sunday's theme is the fellowship of the Holy Spirit and our being sent forth to be the church wherever we are. Sunday begins in the joy of the Resurrection on the third day as we are raised to life with morning wake up. The "Humanness of Jesus" meditation in morning chapel sets the tone for the day, reminding us that God used Jesus' human qualities and can use our human qualities to convey the grace and goodness of God in everyday life

CHANGING OUR WORLD

The talk on CHANGING OUR WORLD challenges us to make a personal plan to bring the love of Christ to bear in ourselves, our families, our work settings, our friendships, and our community.

Atmosphere: Hopefully, all pilgrims have experienced a change of heart. Some who have come to the weekend as substantial Christians are now aware that they could do much more for Jesus Christ. Generally, all pilgrims are ready to go out and take action to advance God's reign.

SANCTIFYING GRACE

The SANCTIFYING GRACE talk conveys the mystery of the Holy Spirit's ongoing work of maturing us in the love of Christ as we practice God's presence and serve Christ in the world.

Atmosphere: The pilgrims have gained an awareness that this event is just the beginning. Their spiritual lives will grow and deepen, and they will acquire new insights into Christian living. Their practices of piety also will change and take on new forms to keep pace with their spiritual growth.

BODY OF CHRIST

The BODY OF CHRIST talk calls us as disciples to be the hands and feet of the risen Christ together, the corporate extension of Christ's life and ministry today, through our local churches and the larger Christian family.

Atmosphere: Many pilgrims will be enthusiastic about going home. Others may feel troubled about living the life in grace in an un-Christian world. A basic problem is that people think of themselves as individuals. This talk moves the pilgrims to think of themselves as part of a small, closely knit group intensely living out the Christian life.

PERSEVERANCE

The PERSEVERANCE talk offers both a method and encouragement for living in grace during the rest of our lives through the mutual support and guidance of an accountability group.

Atmosphere: Pilgrims evidence conspicuous joy and an interest in what will happen tomorrow. They desire to do the Lord's work. A concern about how to continue this feeling of God's presence after they leave the event may surface. Many feel saturated by ideas, so keep the talk simple and to the point.

FOURTH DAY

The FOURTH DAY talk sends us forth with the challenge to live every day hereafter as a continuation of the Emmaus event by keeping the fire of Christ's love burning and by maintaining close contact with Christ and Christian friends through church, accountability groups, and the Emmaus Community.

Atmosphere: Many of the pilgrims will be thinking of going home. Yet a strong undercurrent of concern about persevering in living the Fourth Day may arise. The simple rule to follow is this: "Contact with Christ and contact with our brothers and sisters." Through personal testimony, the speaker has shown that a person can live and grow in the life of grace throughout the Fourth Day of his or her life.

Preparing for Completion

After the FOURTH DAY talk, the Spiritual Director begins to prepare the pilgrims for the completion of the event by reviewing the take-home information in the packets, answering questions about Emmaus, and reinforcing the "Points to Remember" that focus on the attitude with which we return to our homes and churches. The Spiritual Director then introduces the personal agape letters. The Assistant Lay Directors distribute the envelopes to the pilgrims who remain in the conference room. When they have had sufficient time to read their letters, the pilgrims line up by tables for a special commissioning service in which each receives an Emmaus cross and an accountability group card as a reminder of his or her responsibility as a Christian to share Christ's love with the world. The pilgrims then go to the chapel for Closing, where the Emmaus Community greets them in song. The pilgrims may share how these three days have influenced them, and then all are invited to celebrate Holy Communion as part of the extended Christian family.

Initiating Morning Wake Up

Each morning a bell or music may awaken the pilgrims, but the upbeat spirit of Sunday morning wake up time focuses especially on starting the day as disciples of a risen Lord. The pilgrims have journeyed a long way since Thursday night. They have heard Jesus' message; they have known his presence; and many have committed themselves anew to him. They have experienced God's amazing grace again and again, most recently in the Community's extraordinary display of love in Candlelight the night before. On Sunday morning, team members may awaken the pilgrims with singing and the strumming of guitars outside their cabins or doors, a joyful reminder that God has made them new persons in Christ. The pilgrims rise to the new day in the spirit of Resurrection as members of the risen body of Christ. Sunday morning wake up launches day three with the enthusiasm that characterizes Christian life.

Sunday morning wake up is the team's responsibility. Some team members get out of bed early, organize a troupe of singers, and serenade the pilgrims from outside their door or cabin a few minutes before wake-up time.

Introducing the Accountability Group (Group Reunion)

On Sunday afternoon when the pilgrims are tired and less than eager for a fourteenth talk, the Lay Director has the difficult but significant task of introducing the pilgrims to the accountability group as a means of living in grace for the rest of their lives. During the team preview of the PERSEVERANCE talk, the team listens to help the Lay Director effectively communicate the value of the accountability group and clearly describe the intended process. The Lay Director's own experience with the value of the accountability group supports the message.

The Lay Director can prepare the Table Leaders during team meetings for the accountability group discussion at the tables following the PERSEVERANCE talk. Table Leaders will reinforce the value of the accountability groups with their own experience. Those with limited experience will have been encouraged to form accountability groups during team formation to learn from the experience of other team members. The table discussion reinforces the talk.

Another option is to offer a three-to-five-minute role play of an accountability group during the PERSEVERANCE talk. When called upon by the Lay Director, three team members move their chairs to the front and demonstrate the simplicity of the process. They can open their meeting with the Prayer to the Holy Spirit, each responding to one part of the accountability group card and one of the questions. They then remember others in need and close with prayer. The actors rehearse ahead of time, prepare honest but succinct responses to the questions, avoid out-of-character comments and explanations, and then quickly return to their tables so the Lay Director can continue the talk. The Lay Director takes responsibility to recruit team members for this role play, since this is part of his or her talk.

After the talk, the table discussion could model a group instead of simply talking about accountability groups. Table Leaders explain the process by leading it. At the end of three spiritually rich days, the pilgrims have much to share in response to some of the questions on the card. By having them "group" with their friends, their first experience will surely be positive. They will be more likely to want to continue such meetings as part of their Fourth Day.

Reviewing the Pilgrims' Information Packet

Immediately after the FOURTH DAY talk, the Assistant Lay Directors pass out the pilgrims' take-home packets, and the Spiritual Director reviews the contents: pilgrim and team rosters, group photo, book list, a volunteer sheet, "Points to Remember," and Upper Room devotional materials. The Spiritual Director leads the group in correcting names and addresses and turns to "Points to Remember."

"Points to Remember" allows the Spiritual Director to note some problems Emmaus pilgrims may encounter when they return to their churches. Reviewing "Points to Remember" offers them help on how best to direct their enthusiasm. The Spiritual Director also has a last chance to answer questions about Emmaus, to reinforce its purpose, and to say whatever remains to be said about the proper attitude for reentry into the world. The Spiritual Director urges the pilgrims to return to their churches with deeds of love and acts of humble service.

Introducing Individual Agape Letters

When the "Points to Remember" and the packets have been reviewed, the Spiritual Director introduces the individual agape letters as a final act of agape. The individual agape letters are another, more penetrating reminder that the pilgrims are loved, not only by the people with them on the Walk who have not known them long and people far away who do not know them at all, but by persons who know them best and to whom they will return very soon.

Paul's letters, written as acts of love, often began with such words as, "May God our Father and the Lord Jesus Christ give you grace and peace." The intent of the letters that the pilgrims receive now is that God, through the love behind the words, will give them grace and peace.

The Assistant Lay Directors distribute the envelopes containing each pilgrim's personal agape letters, and the pilgrims receive about thirty minutes to read them. Team members tend to their own letters and give the pilgrims personal space to read without interruption or commentary from curious observers. The pilgrims also need time to read their letters without being rushed. Therefore, the leaders carefully watch the clock and maintain the schedule on Sunday, not only to be on time for closing but to guard the reserved block of time in the schedule for reading the letters.

Personal agape letters are letters written to individual pilgrims by close friends and family members. More important than the number of letters is the quality. Sponsors aim to get eight to twelve letters. An avalanche of letters can be overwhelming and difficult to receive. Furthermore, fifty letters for one pilgrim can present an obstacle to the message of grace for the lonely pilgrim who receives only five letters and does not understand why. Sponsors may give their pilgrims additional letters after closing. When a pilgrim has more letters than he or she can read in thirty minutes, the agape team stacks the letters so that those from closest relatives are on top and will be read first.

The leadership discourages team members from writing letters to pilgrims during the event because preoccupation with letter writing will keep them from being truly present to the pilgrims. A meaningful time for team members to write the pilgrims is *after* the event. A note of appreciation lets the pilgrims know that the friendships they formed did not stop at the end of event, and it supports them in their Fourth Day.

Presenting the Accountability Group Card and Emmaus Cross

After thirty minutes of letter-reading time, the pilgrims are called together in the conference room or a chapel other than the one that will host closing. During this time of consecration, they will receive their Emmaus crosses and accountability group cards as reminders of their responsibility as Christians. This activity also gives the pilgrims and team an opportunity to bring closure to the three days and to express their feelings to one another before being swallowed up in the Emmaus Community at Closing.

In preparation for this event, the Assistant Lay Directors hang the pilgrims' Emmaus crosses over the edge of an altar table or over the arms of a table cross or through holes in a large standing cross that has been made for this purpose. They also cluster the accountability group cards (on which the pilgrims have written their names) in stacks by tables. After the pilgrims line up or sit by table groups, the Spiritual Director addresses them with the explanation and instructions for this service (given in the *Walk to Emmaus 3-Day Schedule*). If the crosses have been a symbolic focus of prayer for the Community on the pilgrims' behalf throughout the weekend in the Prayer Chapel, tell the pilgrims that. Following the order of the accountability group cards, the Spiritual Director calls forward a table group and then each member by name. The Spiritual Director presents each pilgrim with his or her accountability group card and the Lay Director presents the cross, putting it around the neck while stating the words, "Christ is counting on you." Each pilgrim responds with the words, "And I am counting on Christ."

In the Spiritual Director's instructions for this service, he or she asks the Table Leaders and team members to step aside and form a receiving line around the room. At this time, the team members may put on their crosses. As the pilgrims receive their accountability group cards and crosses, they return to their seats by table. When all the pilgrims have received cards and crosses, they form a circle with the team, and the Clergy and Lay Directors go to the head of the receiving line and greet each person. Those who have been greeted then follow the directors in doing likewise until everyone makes the complete circle.

When the time for Closing arrives, the Clergy and Lay Directors usually conclude this final time together as a conference room family by inviting everyone to join hands, then offering a prayer, and singing a song such as "They'll Know We Are Christians." The pilgrims then receive instructions for going to Closing and sitting by tables and are reminded to think about the two questions to which they may respond: "What has the weekend meant to me?" and "What do I intend to do about it?"

Attending Closing

The Assistant Lay Directors lead the pilgrims to the chapel for Closing where the Emmaus Community greets them with enthusiastic singing. Closing is more than a family party; it is a summation of the entire event. The pilgrims have walked with the Lord, heard the Lord's message, and experienced the Lord's presence in many ways. Here, at journey's end, they have their first opportunity to tell the Community what has happened to them on the road and how they recognized Jesus in the breaking of the bread, just as the two disciples told their friends when they returned to Jerusalem. (See Luke 24:33-35.)

The pilgrims enter the chapel wearing their crosses, acknowledged members of the Emmaus Community who have taken the three-day walk. They take their seats *in the front rows with the Emmaus Community.* Closing celebrates what has taken place; it is not a graduation. Closing includes a welcome of the pilgrims as members of the Emmaus Community, a brisk set of introductions, the witness of the pilgrims, introduction of the Community Lay Director for Fourth Day announcements and comments, introduction of the Community Spiritual Director for presentation of the Emmaus hand cross to the Lay Director on behalf of the Community, and a final celebration of Holy Communion.

The Lay Director conducts Closing until the introduction of the Community Lay Director. The Lay Director can improve the quality of Closing by giving clear instructions about the witness of the new Emmaus Community members, as follows.

Prior to Closing, the Lay Director will have reminded the pilgrims to contemplate the two questions to which they may respond: "What has the weekend meant to me?" and "What do I intend to do about it?" After introductions, the Lay Director states the questions again: (1) "What has this weekend meant to me?" and (2) "What do I intend to do about it?" The questions are taped to the lectern as well. The Lay Director reminds the pilgrims that this time is for response to the two questions. The Lay Director asks two team members to model answers and set the tone for the pilgrims. These two spiritually mature team members understand the form of witness they are to model. The Lay Director reminds the two team members to answer the questions as they pertain *to the current weekend*. Previous Emmaus event experiences, while meaningful to the team members, have no relation to the current pilgrims.

The celebrant for the closing service of Holy Communion can improve and shorten Closing by making his or her Communion meditation brief, usually stressing one point that takes about five minutes to explicate. The pilgrims' own testimonies have borne witness to the Word. Lengthy sermons are unnecessary and inconsiderate of the Community. Traditionally, the Community Spiritual Director serves as celebrant for the closing service of Holy Communion. Closing is a Community event and the Community Spiritual Director's leadership represents the welcome of the larger Emmaus Community and the pilgrims' entry into its membership. Sometimes the Community Spiritual Director or the Board of Directors will assign this responsibility to the Walks Spiritual Director if the Community Spiritual Director is unavailable.

GENERAL REMARKS

Leaning into the Fourth Day

Each day of the Walk leans into the next, and all three lean into the Fourth Day. Thursday night's solitary reflections and preparations conclude the following day in morning chapel when the "walking" begins. Friday's emphasis on God and God's initiative of grace begins to lean into Saturday's focus on response to grace through Friday's JUSTIFYING GRACE talk, the LIFE OF PIETY talk, and the Emmaus Road prayer experience.

Saturday's activities, which emphasize response to the grace of Jesus Christ, begin to lean into Sunday's focus on the Christian community in action, during and after Candlelight. In Candlelight, the pilgrims experience the outreach of the Christian community on their behalf and recommit their lives as disciples in that community.

Sunday's activities focus on the community of the Holy Spirit being Christ in the world and open onto Monday and every Fourth Day thereafter. *The aim of Emmaus is to strengthen pilgrims for living their Fourth Day.* This message needs to be clearly understood on Sunday. Leaders guide the Walk to Emmaus with a Fourth Day perspective.

Communities and teams sometimes unconsciously emphasize the powerful events of Dying Moments Communion and Candlelight, thereby diminishing the impact and effectiveness of later Fourth Day messages about accountability groups, church renewal, and involvement of the pilgrims in the Emmaus Community.

Each experience on a Walk to Emmaus while critical, remains in perspective with God's guidance of the pilgrims through the total experience of the Walk. The Fourth Day for the Emmaus Community is not simply time between events to prepare for more events but time to work as Christian disciples and to support one another as active Christians in the church and everyday environments. The arena of lasting transformation is not a single event but daily life in the world with God. What shapes lives most in the long run is not a single mountaintop experience but the resulting relationships with other Christians who decide to meet, pray, study, and support one another's struggle to live lives of faith, hope, and love.

Keeping the Schedule

Each step along the way on a Walk to Emmaus carries significance. The schedule, like a trusted map, directs the leaders and assures them that they are all on the same walk, no matter who does the navigation.

The schedule allows time for each step, which assures the pilgrims enough time to experience the whole walk. When leaders reallocate time, they may be making a value judgment about which parts of the event are more important based on their own experience and needs. Granting more time for the pilgrims to experience one part of the journey may mean rushing past another meaningful part for pilgrims with different needs. The schedule keeps the pilgrims moving at a reasonable pace and balances their use of time for the sake of the whole experience.

The schedule also considers the need for pilgrims to take breaks and to rest. The Walk to Emmaus is not a marathon or long-distance march with the aim of wearing down the pilgrims until they break. Leaders with this intention do not represent faith in the power of God's presence in people's lives, nor do they respect the dignity of the pilgrims. Further, they do a disservice to the Emmaus movement. A Walk to Emmaus has a full agenda, is intense at points, and can be emotionally tiring even without the well-intentioned but misguided help of leaders who want to stretch it out further. Leaders respect the pilgrims' need for occasional unstructured time and work to protect the allotted time for breaks, recreation, reflection, and rest so the pilgrims remain alert and refreshed.

The schedule serves as a guide, a discipline, and a goal. The event works best when leaders adhere to the schedule. Yet those who try to maintain a rigid schedule down to the minute will experience frustration and may also frustrate the pilgrims.

While Walk to Emmaus leaders need to be firm about the schedule, they maintain enough flexibility that the pilgrims do not feel pressured and regimented. Sometimes the pilgrims may require a few more minutes to discuss a talk; at other times, they may need less time and will sit idle and bored unless leaders notice and respond. A large group of pilgrims will require more time for Communion, sharing with the entire group, and moving from place to place. Sometimes special needs arise that command the attention of team members and delay the event. In these cases, the leadership calls upon the Walk to Emmaus Spiritual Directors to fulfill their pastoral role rather than hold up the event indefinitely.

The pilgrims' response time to the bell tends to become slower as the Walk to Emmaus progresses. Some simply stop hearing the bell. During team meetings, remind the team members to encourage promptness by example and to echo to persons around them the call to the conference room when the bell rings.

Sensitivity of the Walk to Emmaus leadership to the needs of the moment allows for wise adjustments to the schedule. If the walk falls behind schedule, the event leader looks ahead for places to save time and while protecting necessary scheduled blocks of time, such as the time to read individual agape letters and the scheduled long break. If the walk runs ahead of schedule, the leaders avoid imposing more structured activity on the pilgrims. The Walk to Emmaus leaders can give the pilgrims more free-time to be alone, to visit informally and develop relationships, to sing, or to further discuss and consider responses to the talks.

Tone of Each Day and Team Disposition

Since the team members already know one another well and have journeyed far together as a Community, they will need to tone down their natural exuberance and enjoyment of being together to a level that the pilgrims find comfortable. Let the pilgrims get to know one another gradually and give them the freedom to move at their own pace. The pilgrims need space to reflect on what is happening and to begin to trust the leaders. As the walk progresses and the Spirit begins to move, team members express sensitivity to the developing sense of community by encouraging a deeper level of sharing and outward support for one another. Always, the team members set the tone by participating in a natural, joyful, and wholehearted manner, thus exhibiting the qualities of authentic piety.

Paying attention to the team's tone involves perceiving the time it takes to establish relationships and develop trust, avoiding aggressive Christian behavior on the part of the team, and cooperating with the initiative of the Holy Spirit in fostering spiritual community among the pilgrims. Team members avoid contriving moods or manipulating the emotional atmosphere. They are not actors who dramatize the change from a cool and distant disposition at the start of the walk to a warm and joyous disposition at the end. The design of a Walk to Emmaus provides an environment in which the pilgrims can authentically experience God's gift of life together in Christ. Because the leaders trust Christ to be present on the Walk to Emmaus, they need not imitate or fabricate gifts of the event, only receive and share.

The Emmaus model has a rationale for distributing agape during a Walk to Emmaus and for distributing the personal agape letters last. As the event unfolds, the agape becomes progressively personal. A wave of agape love that surprisingly intensifies during the unfolding event washes over the pilgrims. Early in the event, the introduction of general agape communicates God's love for everyone primarily through Community prayer and sacrifice. Attention remains focused on the Community letters and the event Prayer Vigil. Next, the pilgrims become especially aware of table agape. Table agape, while the same for everyone, shows up as a gift for each person, reflecting the fact that God loves us all the same but cares for each of us individually. Near the end of the event, the agape letters from family and friends communicate God's love for each pilgrim in personal ways through relationships that are unique and unrepeatable.

Other reasons exist for waiting until near the end of the walk to distribute the individual agape letters. The letters are part of the end-of-event reentry process. They come at a time when the pilgrims feel the Walk to Emmaus is closing and the giving has surely ended. The letters show the pilgrims that, though they may be tired and the event is almost over, God is not finished loving them and will continue to do so through the people in their lives. The letters prepare them to return with gratitude to a world with people who appreciate and provide support for them. The letters also serve as examples of Christian action as the pilgrims are sent forth to share with others the grace they have received. The personal letters enrich the final part of the walk and make personal the summary message of being the church wherever pilgrims find themselves, which is the goal of Emmaus.

Above all, the distribution of the individual agape letters near the event's end supports the concept of the Walk to Emmaus as a time set apart from usual patterns and relationships in which the pilgrims can sort out and reestablish their relationship with God. At the start of the walk, the pilgrims just begin to let go of their focus on relationships back home and to turn their attention to a deeper relationship with God. Early on, some may struggle as they question why they are there, learn the rhythm of the walk, and begin to get a fresh perspective on their lives.

Particularly for the cloistered three-day event of the Walk to Emmaus, team members may have an unfounded fear that pilgrims will leave early unless they are opened up emotionally by receiving their personal letters early. The intent of the letters is not to improve pilgrims' feelings about the Emmaus event or to influence them to stay for the duration. The letters are part of the progression of agape, moving from general to specific and then to personal.

Likewise, at other times during a Walk to Emmaus, receiving personal letters would shift the focus and likely crowd an already full and emotionally charged schedule with more. Letters from loved ones at any time will be a good experience and provide a lift, but they do not necessarily serve the design of the Walk to Emmaus. Generating an emotional high or a particular atmosphere for the pilgrims' community is not the purpose of the personal letters. The letters help the pilgrims realize that they are loved, not only in the community, but by people in the world to which they are returning.

THE LEARNING PROCESS

The methodology of talk, silence, and discussion (as well as summaries, representations, and sharing in the evening) is a learning process integral to Emmaus that makes it possible for everyone to participate. The silence provides time for everyone to meditate on the content of the message before talking about it during the discussion time. Creating representations can bring out the best in both the talkers and the doers, those more attuned to concepts and those more attuned to images, and can encourage each to learn through the strengths of the other. Real learning not only results from new rational understandings but from changes in people's operating images of themselves, life, and God. The summary representation time provides an opportunity for pilgrims to invent their own images for holding and appropriating the truth they receive on their Walk to Emmaus.

The Walk to Emmaus requires each table to present joint summaries and posters, skits, or songs in the evening, challenging the pilgrims to work together on common tasks and to become a community of persons who respect one another's gifts and uniquenesses. Sharing all summaries and the representations at once in the evening provides a way to reinforce the main ideas and images of the whole day's message, while having fun as an entire Community. The total process intends to facilitate both informational and formational learning, to stimulate rich dialogue and interaction, and to foster development of relationships at the tables around a common task.

Honoring the Community-Building Process

Over the course of the Walk to Emmaus, the many individuals in the conference room—team and pilgrims alike—become a community of faith. Because the Holy Spirit needs the space and time to build the community and to weave the pilgrims together in love, the pilgrims are generally cloistered for the duration of the event. The pilgrims enjoy freedom of expression, openness, and intimacy as they grow in their trust, love, and understanding of one another by the grace of God. This community experience offers a glimpse of the abundant life Christ came to give and a vision of what the church is meant to be.

To preserve the cloistered atmosphere of the experience, people other than the Conference Room Team have no contact with the pilgrims during the walk. The obvious exceptions to this rule are the parts of the walk that include members of the Emmaus Community: Candlelight, meal servers, etc. Even in these instances, the Community members are present only in their servant roles to do their part. They do not enter into casual relationship with the pilgrims. Community members do not enter the conference room to hear a talk or to mix with the pilgrims. Leaders remind the team members and pilgrims ahead of time that no talks, table dialogues, or other parts of the event will be recorded. Boards will ensure that no part of the Walk to Emmaus experience will be videotaped, electronically recorded, or photographed. Talks will not be broadcast outside the conference room.

Baptism and the Emmaus Weekend

No one performs baptisms during a Walk to Emmaus. Baptism for youth and adults is a sign of God's unconditional love and the individual's conscious acceptance of his or her membership in the body of Christ as it finds expression through some specific congregation or denomination. Emmaus is not a church or a denomination. It complements and supports—not replaces—ongoing church ministries in helping persons grow as disciples. If persons were baptized on Emmaus events, then the Emmaus Community would function as a church body to which Christians belong; the Walk Spiritual Director would play a role that belongs to a pilgrim's pastor.

When pilgrims seek baptism on a Walk to Emmaus, the walk Spiritual Director counsels with them about the affirmation of faith they desire to make, helps them decide how best to act on it after the walk, and supports them in doing so. If the request for baptism surfaces as a common issue in a Community, it raises a question about the quality of the Community's sponsorship. Are sponsors inviting active Christians to enhance their spiritual formation (which is the purpose of Emmaus), or are they sponsoring non-Christians for their conversion?

THREE-DAY OVERVIEW

Day 1	Day 2	Day 3
God Proclamation/Call Divine Invitation	*The Lord Jesus Christ* Conversion Our Response	*The Holy Spirit* Consecration Christian Life in Mission
Morning Meditation **THE LOVING FATHER** **(Prodigal Son)** God loves us unconditionally and longs for our return.	**Morning Meditation** **FOUR RESPONSES TO CHRIST** In view of these, how will we respond to Christ?	**Morning Meditation** **HUMANNESS OF JESUS** God uses our humanness to touch this world with grace.
PRIORITY Human beings are shaped by a unique capacity to make decisions about their priorities. What is your priority?	**GROW THROUGH STUDY** New life in Christ involves growing through study of scripture, tradition, and our world (giving our mind to God).	**CHANGING OUR WORLD** Disciples will transform their environments by being a Christian presence in the four fields of ministry.
PREVENIENT GRACE God's love searches us out, seeks to redeem humanity, and wants to give us a life in grace.	**MEANS OF GRACE** This new life in Christ is made real by means of sacraments and other sacred moments in which we celebrate Christ's overcoming death in our lives.	**SANCTIFYING GRACE** Disciples continue to grow in the grace of Christ through obedience to the Holy Spirit in the disciplines of prayer and service.
PRIESTHOOD OF ALL BELIEVERS God's love is shared by Christians called to be the church—to be priests to one another, a channel of grace between God and people.	**CHRISTIAN ACTION** This new life is expressed by sharing Christ as a friend with friends—giving one's hands and feet to God, both in the church and in the world.	**BODY OF CHRIST** Disciples are called together to be the body of Christ, joining their gifts for ministry and mission to "the least of these."

Day 1	Day 2	Day 3
JUSTIFYING GRACE By God's grace, we are accepted and set right with God in Jesus Christ. New life in Christ comes when we say yes to God's offer of grace.	**OBSTACLES TO GRACE** This new life is not free from obstacles of sin, but grace and discipline enable us to overcome obstacles and grow through them.	**PERSEVERANCE** Disciples of Jesus cannot make it alone but can persevere with strength from the Spirit through mutual support in accountability groups.
LIFE OF PIETY This new life is rooted in a living relationship with God, sustained by grace through spiritual disciplines—giving one's heart to God.	**DISCIPLESHIP** This new life is discipleship, life lived in grace, following in Jesus' footsteps, growing in his likeness—giving heart, head, and hands to God.	**FOURTH DAY** The three days are over, but Day Four begins. This is Emmaus's purpose: a lifetime of discipleship, bringing new life to our churches and conveying grace where we live.
Day 1 Focus Is about God's gracious offer to us of a relationship and of a new life centered in Jesus Christ.	**Day 2 Focus** Is about Christ as model for our response to that gracious offer and our living in grace as disciples through practicing the means of grace.	**Day 3 Focus** Is about the Holy Spirit's strategy for bringing new life and transformation to our world through us and our ongoing participation in that mission as the church.

SECTION 5— PREPARING YOUR TALK

THE MESSAGE OF EMMAUS

The talks given during the Walk to Emmaus are the principal vehicle that communicates the message of the event. The talks are the thread that weaves through chapel times, posters, discussions, and personal contacts.

Your talk joyfully proclaims the good news of Jesus' saving action; you present it in a manner that will draw persons closer to Christ. You proclaim it with conviction! Your invitation to give this talk presumes that you are living the doctrine/ideal you will present.

Your talk bears witness to your experience of the truths you proclaim. You can witness only to what you know to be true in your own life. Therefore, remember the following:

What is not studied is not known, and what is not known cannot be communicated; what is not lived is not experienced, and what is not experienced cannot be shared.

After prayerful consideration, the Team Selection Committee has asked you to give a specific talk. You may feel uncomfortable with the talk topic or feel unable to prepare it effectively. If this is the case, don't hesitate to say so. For example, if study of the scriptures isn't your strong suit or you aren't familiar with the broad spectrum of Christian literature and authors, don't agree to give the GROW THROUGH STUDY talk. The text of a talk—your complete, personal possession of a talk—is based on prayer, study, knowledge, and experience.

Your talk is one element in the Emmaus event. While critical to the event's progression, your talk is not your only responsibility—or even your major responsibility. Your talk presents one element of a carefully designed short course in Christian living. Consider all the talks of the event as one talk, of which you present one part. You may refer to a previous talk to reinforce a point (such as, "Yesterday, Mary said such and such about worship"), but you fit your talk into the progression of the other talks. Your talk will include all the major points in the outline and only those points.

Your talk's success depends on your availability as an instrument of the Holy Spirit in its preparation.

POINTS TO REMEMBER

1. Each talk intends to accomplish two things:

   a) To present clearly a part of the short course in Christianity;

   b) To inspire the pilgrims to act on what is presented.

2. Your talk goes far beyond simply presenting some good and useful ideas. Its purpose is to say things that must be said.

3. Your talk employs clear, concise language that falls within the grasp of all present. All the listeners, from the least educated or spiritually immature person to those who have a firm grasp on Jesus' hand, can understand your concepts. Keep in mind you want to move your audience along. Give them enough to move them on to something they have not experienced or thought before. A well-balanced talk will have something for everyone.

4. Each talk leads in a definite direction. Remain aware of this direction at all times. Each talk progresses from low key on the first day to a high key on the third day. Keep your talk in the proper perspective with those before and after it. Give the pilgrims a clear road to follow without thrusting them to a high point before they are ready.

   The entire team takes responsibility to see that each talk fits the pattern regarding the progression in intensity or strength.

BODY OF CHRIST

Sunday

DISCIPLESHIP

Saturday

LIFE OF PIETY

Friday

5. Your personal witness serves to illustrate a point in the talk, not glorify the speaker. Personal witness will take less than one-third of the total talk time.

THE LOGISTICS OF PREPARING YOUR TALK

Here are some basic principles or guidelines to follow when preparing a talk.

1. Begin now—don't put it off until the last minute.

2. Base your talk on the Walk to Emmaus Talk Outlines. Present the points as outlined using your own words and your own experience. Read and reflect on the outline and the language of the talk you are to give. Become familiar with the flow and intent of the thoughts in the outline. Check the scripture references in their context to the principal message of the talk.

3. Serve the purpose of the Emmaus event and make a positive contribution by remaining faithful to the outline provided and comprehending it well. If you do, the pilgrims will understand the presentation.

4. Have a good grasp of the subject as you prepare your talk. Use your talk outline and the description of the three days. Know how your talk builds the Walk to Emmaus; know its relationship to the other talks.

5. Follow the outline and resolve any difficulties you may experience with your Lay Director or Spiritual Director. The talk is you—your work and your words. "Witness talks" offer first-person experiences not detached observations. You will find yourself living that which you are preparing; examine your own life in light of the subject. Use this examination constructively for the needs of your talk.

6. Pray that the Holy Spirit reveals the manner in which you can best witness to the truths your talk communicates. Ask your family and reunion group to pray that God will help you deliver the talk so God's message goes out through your words.

7. Do not exceed the time assigned. Each talk is to be no more than twenty to twenty-five minutes. The one exception is the MEANS OF GRACE talk, which is allotted thirty-five to forty-five minutes.

8. Make your own outline, in which you work to make the points in the Walk to Emmaus Talk Outline give voice to the personal witness you might use.

9. Keep in mind that an effective talk depends on its:
   - objective—the main points of the outline
   - style—the manner in which it is to be given
   - situation—how it relates to the other talks, especially the one before and after it
   - environment—the general feeling of the pilgrims at the time it is given
   - technique—how the material is presented

10. Ask a Spiritual Director or experienced leader to assist you if you feel unsure. (The Lay Director can suggest someone.) Notes from previous weekends or former speakers provide good resources.

11. Don't confuse the talk with too many details and examples. Make sure the main points stand out. Use examples with care, bringing to bear only those that explain a point.

12. Spend time with your own notes. Don't be in a hurry to complete them too early. Plan any visual aids you choose to use.

13. Keep in mind that the pilgrims will be taking notes, so give them time. Build in "repeats" of important points. Plan to incorporate key points in your visual aids.

14. Allow your own natural humor to come through in your talk. However, feel no need to find a joke just for the sake of a light remark—strained humor strains the listeners' understanding.

15. Write out the talk in manuscript form. This ensures the preview talk will match the weekend talk. Type talks out in double- or triple-spaced format. Keep the talk in a ring binder or orderly stack. Mark your key words; punctuate your talk properly; and follow the punctuation when you give your talk.

---

16. Keep your vocabulary simple and avoid specialized terms that are hard to pronounce. They also are hard to hear. Employ terms that you define in the course of your talk. Stay away from terms or expressions that require a definition that becomes a side remark to your talk. Speak in your own words and, except when directly quoting an author, avoid paraphrasing words from your reading and study.

17. Structure sentences and paragraphs so you can speak a sentence without pausing for breath in the middle. If the talk requires a longer sentence, build in natural pauses for emphasis and for breathing. Keep your paragraphs on one subject; don't jumble thoughts around in one paragraph. This focus will improve your delivery and the understanding of the pilgrims.

18. Refer to previous talks: who (his/her name) said what (in what talk) and when (yesterday, this morning), such as, "Do you remember what Don said in the Life of Piety talk last night about . . . ?" Build on it in your talk.

19. Implement "power phrases." What do you want the pilgrims to remember? What can they "grab onto" for the activities and discussion that follow your talk?

20. Appendix C provides helpful information about why the use of handouts is discouraged.

THE USE OF SCRIPTURE

The New Testament serves as the primary source of the message of Emmaus. Use it! However, an excessive citing of scripture will detract from the naturalness of your talk. Limit your scripture references to two or three and write them out in your manuscript so that you do not have to flip back and forth through your Bible. Be sure you understand the proper context of the scriptures you choose. Check with a Spiritual Director if in doubt.

PERSONAL WITNESS

Balancing personal witness and the message of the talk is difficult. Remember, the message is essential; personal witness only illustrates or amplifies a point. It serves to describe what you have just told them. Be careful not to glorify yourself or your relationship with Jesus or to overdo the Holy Spirit's movement in your life.

Avoid using your personal witness to trigger an emotional response in the pilgrims. Let the tears on a weekend result from the Holy Spirit's working in the pilgrims. Attempting to manipulate emotions from the lectern shifts the pilgrims' focus *to* you and *away* from the message of the talk. No one denies that tears will occur. Don't build an emotional experience into a talk just for effect.

Never use personal witness to point out another's transgression, especially a family member. We all belong to one family; the talk is not the setting to air grievances. Adhere to this principle strictly, even if your point is valid and relevant to the message. Find another example of personal witness.

PERSONAL REHEARSAL OF YOUR TALK

1. Complete the talk and read it aloud to yourself. Mark obvious errors on the copy as you read. Identify problems for a rewrite. How well do the thoughts hold together? In what ways do the thoughts transition smoothly from one to another? How does it sound?

2. Rewrite and rewrite. Use wide spacing; underlining; margin notes; highlighters to indicate key words, pauses, repeats.

3. Read your talk aloud until it's so familiar you can speak from key words.

4. Now, give the talk aloud. Give it as though you were delivering it to the pilgrims. Have something to serve as a lectern as you practice. Stand up to practice. Remember what the conference room looks like, where the pilgrims sit. Give your talk to them. Be natural. Role play by employing all the gestures and animation you would use. Become comfortable with your words, gestures, and audience in the quiet of your own home. Some team members tape their practice, then listen to the tape while following the manuscript, marking the poorly delivered or poorly thought-out parts for correction.

5. Time your talk as you rehearse it aloud in your home to fit the allotted time.

6. Correct errors and weak spots.

7. Now, give your talk again and again according to steps 4 and 5 above. Your talk will be polished by the time you review it for the team. The team members expect to know and have the right to know exactly what you intend to say on the weekend. Knowing the content of your talk is essential in critiquing the talk. Remember, talks are the work of the whole team.

OFFERING YOUR TALK TO THE TEAM

1. Prepare a final draft of your text in manuscript form. Never use an outline to give your talk. This will ensure that the talk you give at the team critique will be that same talk you present on the weekend.

2. Come to the team meeting with a fully completed talk and posters or visual aids.

3. At the completion of your talk preview, the team members will critique your talk and delivery. You may think an idea, story, or thought is wonderful, but the team may believe it is inappropriate. When this happens, defer to the team's suggestions and change what you have prepared, remembering that you are only a part of one message for that weekend. The team members may offer suggestions to add or remove material to stay within the time limits for each talk.

4. Visual aids are just that: aids to enhance the message. They are not the message; do not allow them to overwhelm the message or the audience. If you choose to use them, keep them simple and to the point.

SECTION 6— PRESENTING YOUR TALK

Few persons on the weekend, except for the clergy, are "professional" speakers. God can and will use you if you desire to serve in this capacity. Persons will have prayed for you a few minutes before you enter the conference room to present your talk. Part of that prayer asks that the Holy Spirit use you to communicate God's truths. God hears these prayers and will be with you as you speak to the pilgrims.

The following prayer may assist you in the process.

Dear Lord, help me as I give this talk. Quiet my spirit; still my apprehension. Instead of the fear I feel, give me your inner peace as I share this talk with the people in the conference room. May I be myself, nothing more, nothing less—simply your child, willing to be used by you. May I sense your presence as I stand before this group, sharing the message that you have given me. I pray that as I share, this group may move closer to you.

I stand in the shadow of your cross; may they see only you. In the name of Jesus I pray. Amen.

STEP INTO YOUR TALK

The easiest way to overcome a feeling of hesitation or uneasiness is to give your talk. Be at peace with yourself and present your witness. Sincerity and lack of pretense will overcome many of the defects you think you have.

Present your talk in a clear, audible, well-paced, and interesting way, making the best use of your God-given talents.

Your personality contributes to the talk. Be yourself, use your own vocabulary, and let the talk reflect the uniqueness of your personality and your walk with Jesus.

Concentrate on the pilgrims, not yourself. Poise will come.

Stand straight with your weight evenly distributed, and face the pilgrims. Don't twist or fidget. Let your feet move a bit. When giving a personal witness, you don't need to use notes.

Don't drape yourself over the lectern; it distracts the pilgrims' attention from the talk. Stay behind the lectern. If you move around, the audience begins to focus on your movement rather than your words. Your movement will diminish the sound quality if you are using a microphone, and persons in various parts of the room will not hear you.

Stiffness and rigidity reflect uncertainty. Take a deep breath, look at your audience, and speak. Concentrate on your talk and you will forget your uneasiness. Remember, you are there to minister to the pilgrims.

HOLD THE ATTENTION OF YOUR AUDIENCE

You have the edge as the speaker because you know your talk and the direction it takes. The talk outline you received provides a road map that leads in the intended direction and any visual aids you use will enhance your talk.

Let the talk flow. Make eye contact with those to whom you speak. Move your eyes from one side of the room to the other, and speak to the individuals sitting at the tables, one person at a time. It is often said, "Your eyes are the windows to your soul." Making eye contact with the pilgrims gives you a glimpse into their souls, and they get a glimpse into yours.

Techniques for Keeping Attention

- Emphasize special points.
- Repeat key points.
- Pause—use the teacher technique of "Now listen closely" to draw them in.
- If you lose your place, relax, find your spot, and carry on.

When you give your talk, remove it from the binder to create a stack of loose sheets that lay flat on the lectern. As you finish one page, simply slide it to the side, moving on to the next page. This approach gives the appearance of a polished talk and speaker.

Dress in good taste. You are there to draw the pilgrim's closer to God.

Finish your talk with a joyful and emphatic "De Colores!" Leave the lectern and your talk notes. An Assistant Lay Director will return the talk to you. Immediately exit the conference room and return to the chapel for a prayer of thanksgiving for what the Holy Spirit accomplished through your talk. Do not return until the tables have completed their discussion and poster time about your talk.

PROBLEMS TO AVOID

1. Talking too long

    Maintaining the integrity and discipline of the weekend requires exact timing on talks. One fruit of the Spirit is self-control, so don't blame the Holy Spirit if you "get on a roll" and can't quit (this may turn out to be ego).

2. Nervous actions

    The jingle of coins, keys, or jewelry detracts from your words and your message. Keep your hands out of your pockets.

3. Lack of eye contact

A fixed stare, looking at the floor, and blank eyes that see no one can distract or annoy. Pacing, walking around, and playing with the microphone will draw more attention than will your message.

LAST BUT NOT LEAST

Please do not study your talk during the event weekend, except for a brief review immediately prior to your presentation.

Remember, your strength is in the Lord.

Trust God for grace and guidance.

Make your Prayer Chapel visit timely and meaningful.

If you have any requests, relay them to one of the Assistant Lay Directors.

SECTION 7—
TEAM MEMBER
RESPONSIBILITIES

Many committees and Fourth-Day activities support an Emmaus event. However, the Emmaus event's Conference Room Team consists of the clergy and six lay positions: Lay Director, Assistant Lay Directors, Music Directors, Board Representative, Table Leaders, and Assistant Table Leaders. Each of these positions has a well-defined role and responsibilities. This chapter describes responsibilities of the first four of these team roles; the "Table Dynamics" section in this manual describes the roles and responsibilities of Table Leader and Assistant Table Leader.

LAY DIRECTOR

The Board of Directors of the local Emmaus Community selects the Lay Director for the Emmaus event. The Lay Director leads the team through team formation and leads the team and pilgrims through the Emmaus event. The Lay Director serves in the employ of the board and is responsible to the board for the conduct of the event. The Lay Director is the principal layperson who, in partnership with the Spiritual Director, directs activities during the Emmaus event.

The Lay Director for a Walk to Emmaus reads and understands the role and responsibilities of the position as presented in the *Walk to Emmaus Directors' Manual* and the following:

1. commits to leading the Walk to Emmaus according to The Upper Room model and under the authority of the board;

2. participates as a member of the Team Selection Committee in the selection of the team for which he/she is the Lay Director;

3. assumes responsibility, along with the Spiritual Director, for conducting team meetings, and for the team-formation process during the weeks preceding the event;

4. is disciplined and acknowledges the authority of the board in setting the rules for the Emmaus team and the conduct of the weekend. The Lay and Spiritual Directors lead the team to a devotionally and disciplined state of preparation;

5. will conduct the Emmaus event in accordance with the schedule of activities, times, and dynamics of the event as presented the *Walk to Emmaus Directors' Manual*;

6. will explain to all prospective team members the after-event follow-up meeting and secure a commitment from them to attend;

7. will secure from all prospective team members a commitment to attend all team meetings (except for health or emergency situations) and to be present during the entire Emmaus event (except for health or emergency situations);

8. provides a final roster of the weekend (team and pilgrims) to the Lay Director of the Community, Registrar, chair of the Team Selection Committee, and the communications team;

9. is responsible for the return of all unused supplies and equipment to the proper place and/or persons;

10. consults with the Board of Directors' representative on the Team as necessary.

ASSISTANT LAY DIRECTORS

Below is the schedule of events and activities for which Assistant Lay Directors (ALDs) take responsibility.

Thursday

Thursday evening following Send-Off and after arrival in the conference room, an Assistant Lay Director invites the pilgrims and team members to pair up with a person they don't know. The partners are to learn a little about each other, including name, church, family, and an interesting fact.

After several minutes, the Assistant Lay Directors will lead the group in sharing about their new friends. Following the introductions, an Assistant Lay Director presents the Spiritual Director, who in turn introduces the Lay Director.

After the Lay Director's talk and before chapel, an Assistant Lay Director announces a short break, bringing everyone back at the sound of the bell.

Be available to answer any questions about medication schedules, smoking areas, and so on.

As the group moves to the chapel, distribute worship booklets to everyone. Count to be sure no one is left behind.

After the pilgrims have gone to bed, remind the team members to go to the team meeting.

Friday

Assistants arise at 6:00 a.m., and, if appropriate, awaken the Kitchen Coordinator.

At 6:30 a.m., wake pilgrims and team members (play music or ring the bell).

At 6:55 a.m., check sleeping quarters for stragglers. In the chapel, count to be sure all are present. Worship will not begin until all show up, except for extenuating circumstances.

Keep the kitchen informed of the time schedule.

At mealtimes, the Assistant Lay Directors make announcements and lead joke time. They ensure the Music Director's guidance for the singing of the meal graces. Remember that the

Friday morning breakfast has a verbal prayer of grace by the Lay Director. The table grace songs are taught midmorning on Friday.

Relay word that a list is available for anyone who forgot a necessary item. Ask about medication schedules. One of the ALDs will follow up on these requests.

An Assistant Lay Director gives the first talk. That person departs breakfast to dress and then goes to the chapel. Another Assistant Lay Director goes to the chapel to pray with the speaker. The Lay Director and the third Assistant prepare the pilgrims in the conference room.

The Assistant Lay Directors are responsible for placing a glass of water on the lectern for each speaker. The Assistant Lay Directors light the candle before each talk and extinguish the candle after each talk. On Friday morning, the Lay Director will light the candle and introduce the speaker.

The three Assistant Lay Directors are also responsible for the following:

Speakers: notify when it is time to get dressed; accompany the speaker to the Prayer Chapel and pray for the speaker; escort the speaker to the conference room; after the talk, escort the speaker back to the Prayer Chapel and pray for the speaker.

Conference room: invite the Music Director to lead the meditative song before each talk; light the candle; introduce the speaker; announce the silent meditation after the talk; extinguish the candle; remove any posters, talk notes, and other visual aids; announce the start of the discussion of the talk on [give the title of the talk each time].

Bell/Schedule: maintains the time schedule for the day, calls the pilgrims and team members to the conference room by ringing the bell.

Note: these three responsibilities will rotate among the three Assistants on a daily basis, remembering that one Assistant will be presenting the first talk on day one and a different Assistant will be presenting the fifteenth talk on day three.

Saturday

Remind the speaker giving the GROW THROUGH STUDY talk to leave the hand cross on the lectern.

After the question-and-answer period about the MEANS OF GRACE talk, have the table groups begin chapel visits for prayer. Each Prayer Chapel visit will last about fifteen minutes. After twelve minutes, quietly enter the chapel and wait for the group to finish.

Sunday

At 6:15 a.m., awaken all the team members who will "sing" the pilgrims awake.

After the first talk, announce that there will be no posters after the talks, only discussion and summaries.

Put the accountability group cards on the tables before the SANCTIFYING GRACE talk.

Distribute the packets. Following the packet explanation, distribute the personal agape letters.

MUSIC DIRECTOR AND ASSISTANT MUSIC DIRECTOR

Prior to the Emmaus event orientation, the Music Director visits the site of the Walk to become familiar with the facility and the available equipment and to learn what rooms will be used for what purpose. The Music Director meets with the Lay and Spiritual Directors to determine the music expectations, both requested and planned.

The Music Directors attend all team meetings to be part of the team-building process, provide music for the team worship services, and play the music that the weekend will employ. They are encouraged to use a variety of media, such as guitar, piano, rhythm instruments, and recorded music. The rehearsal time falls outside the team meeting time.

The Music Directors are to have their instruments tuned and ready to play at all times. They remain in the conference room with the pilgrims.

The following schedule lists specific times for music:

Thursday

10:00 p.m.   Chapel—After the film, Spiritual Director's meditation, and Lay Director's comments, sing or play a meditative solo. The solo serves to enhance the meditation, which focuses on knowing self and where one is on the journey of faith.

Friday

11:00 a.m.   Teach the group a song (a possible selection is "Sing Alleluia to the Lord" from the pilgrims' worship booklet) to introduce talks, "De Colores" (worship booklet), and "Wesley's Grace" (worship booklet). The Music Director or Assistant Music Director explains the history of "De Colores" and the tradition of singing the blessing so pilgrims move beyond simply learning a song to participating in the history of the three-day movement.

• The song "De Colores" has a long-standing tradition in Emmaus and similar three-day programs. This song speaks of God's beauty in the world. According to tradition, people who had experienced the three-day short course in Christianity gave musical expression to their joy of God's love through the words of "De Colores." The words are sung to an old folk tune from Majorca, Spain.

• The tradition of singing grace before and after meals comes from the Benedictines who prayed God's blessing before the meal and thanked God for the blessing of the food and fellowship after the meal.

11:10 a.m.   Lead the group in a song before the Prevenient Grace talk.

1:35 p.m.   Lead the group in a song before the Priesthood of All Believers talk.

2:55 p.m.   Lead the group in a song before the Justifying Grace talk.

5:20 p.m.   Lead pilgrims in singing "De Colores" as they move from the conference room to dining room. Lead singing of grace before and after dinner.

6:15 p.m.   Conference Room—Lead group in a song before the Life of Piety talk.

10:15 p.m.   Meditative solo

Saturday

8:00 a.m.	Lead pilgrims in singing "De Colores" on the way from the chapel to the dining room for breakfast. Lead the group in singing grace before and after breakfast.
8:40 a.m.	Conference Room—Lead the group in a song before the GROW THROUGH STUDY talk.
10:00 a.m.	Teach the pilgrims special songs of response for the Saturday Communion service. Lead the group in a song before the MEANS OF GRACE talk.
12:00 noon	Lead everyone in singing grace before and after lunch.
2:55 p.m.	Conference Room—Lead the group in a song before the CHRISTIAN ACTION talk.
4:25 p.m.	Lead the group in a song before the OBSTACLES TO GRACE talk.
5:40 p.m.	Lead singing of grace before and after dinner.
6:55 p.m.	Conference Room—Lead group in a song before the DISCIPLESHIP talk.
10:00 p.m.	After the Spiritual Director's explanation of Candlelight, lead the group in singing "Jesus, Jesus" as a round.

Sunday

6:45 a.m.	Lead Conference Room Team in wake-up music.
8:00 a.m.	Lead group in singing "De Colores" on the way from the chapel to the dining room. Lead singing of grace before and after breakfast.
8:45 a.m.	Lead group in a song before the CHANGING OUR WORLD talk.
9:55 a.m.	Lead group in a song before the SANCTIFYING GRACE talk.
10:55 a.m.	Lead group in a song before the BODY OF CHRIST talk.
12:00 noon	Lead singing of grace before and after lunch.
1:25 p.m.	Lead group in a song before the PERSEVERANCE talk.
2:25 p.m.	Lead group in a song before the FOURTH DAY talk.
4:15 p.m.	Lead group in singing "They Will Know We Are Christians by Our Love" after the pilgrims receive their Emmaus crosses.
5:00 p.m.	If necessary, provide music for the closing Communion service.

BOARD REPRESENTATIVE

The board appoints a current member to serve on each Emmaus Ministries team. This person monitors but does not direct the weekend and serves as the board advisor if an opinion on procedure is required. The Board Representative observes all that happens and has no other responsibilities. The Board Representative is the same gender as the pilgrims.

SECTION 8— TABLE DYNAMICS

THE IMPORTANCE OF THE TABLE LEADER

Why am I here, Lord?

- I'm here to praise God and to do God's holy work here on earth.

- I'm here to imitate Jesus Christ and to be a window through which the love and grace of Christ can be seen by the pilgrims at this Walk to Emmaus.

- I'm here to pray and make sacrifices for the entire team and pilgrims.

- I'm here to help establish a Christian community by bringing Jesus Christ to this team and pilgrims by accepting the gift of the Holy Spirit.

- I'm here to know the intent of the talks and to help each speaker accomplish the aim of his or her talk by guiding and directing discussion at the table.

- I'm here to display Christian discipleship—to demonstrate love and show my concern for others and accept other persons as individuals.

- I'm here to demonstrate leadership not domination. I do not seek glory for myself but act from loving concern. I'm here as a guide not a counselor. I'm here to listen and to ensure that every person at the table has opportunity to speak.

- I'm here so that when these three days are over, the pilgrims will be able to say of the team members, "I came looking for Christ and found Christ at my table."

- I'm here to ask humbly that God's will, not my will, be done.

- Christ, I'm here to submit my heart and soul to you so your love will grow in me and in each person at my table.

- In all situations I shall ask, "What would Jesus do?"

THE TABLE LEADER

Table Leaders fill a critical role during Emmaus events. Through the Table Leader, many pilgrims will experience, perhaps for the first time, the intimacy, openness, and strength of a small group of Christians in work and prayer. Note this is expressed as *through* the Table Leader, not *because* of the Table Leader. The main dynamics at the table properly will occur among the pilgrims as they learn and experience the ability to be open and prayerful with and for one another. Appendix D offers information on table training.

As a Table Leader, you enable those at the table to experience an effective small-group environment. An open prayerfulness develops among the pilgrims with you in the background. A one-on-one or small-group relationship that focuses on the Table Leader will take much longer than seventy-two hours to develop a small-group relationship. Therefore, the Table Leader fosters this one-on-one relationship among the pilgrims.

The background role isn't as withdrawn as it sounds. It does mean that (1) you are not the center of the growth experience or revelations that occur within your table group; and (2) you are there to be the catalyst by which the small group develops and matures in openness and spiritual community. (A catalyst is an agent that enables a reaction to occur at a faster rate and under more favorable conditions.)

Your role is vital, but you are not the "big cheese," "all that," or the "end all and be all." The question becomes, how do you go about being an effective Table Leader from "the background"?

BUILDING THE SMALL COMMUNITY

Within the overall goal of Emmaus to foster the development of Christian leaders, two supporting goals exist: (1) to create an atmosphere that encourages a desire for a closer walk with Jesus Christ and (2) to involve people in a small Christian group, the accountability group, to create and sustain a spiritual-growth lifestyle.

A Few Pointers Will Help

To serve as a catalyst for a new awareness in another person, you come to the weekend prepared spiritually, emotionally, and physically. A good team member never forgets that he or she is only an instrument through which the Holy Spirit can work, controls his or her emotions and attitudes, and feels rested and physically able to sustain himself or herself through seventy-two demanding hours.

You will get to know each pilgrim at your table personally. You will have a good idea who your table pilgrims are before the end of the last team meeting. You will have some time on Thursday evening before Send-Off and on Friday morning to begin this process. The personal contact with each one of them is significant.

Pilgrims will respond to the Walk to Emmaus in a manner suited to them. Do not expect any of them to respond the way you think they should. There will be as many different concepts of Jesus Christ as are people at the table. Let each one respond to the Walk to Emmaus without overt influence from you. Bear witness to your own belief in Jesus Christ. Let the pilgrims learn by experience.

Remember, this is not your Walk to Emmaus. Your job is to develop a loving, trusting environment in which the pilgrims can grow. Lead the pilgrims into their own discoveries, their own learning. It is critical that on Sunday afternoon they leave feeling strong in a renewed faith they have discovered themselves.

The more the pilgrim feels that he or she is respected as an individual and has the right to decide for himself or herself, the less the pilgrim will resent change.

Be a Christian leader, but do not let the pilgrims depend on you as *the* leader. Encourage them to think. Let them minister to one another, but keep the discussion focused on the talks.

As the Table Leader, you can set the pace. However, if possible, let the pilgrims set the pace. You can monitor what is happening and exert leadership if discussion heads in the wrong direction or bogs down.

Remain open and responsive to all the pilgrims and team members on the weekend, not just to those at your table.

Do not play word games with the pilgrims at your table. Be totally open and honest in everything you say and do.

Team members are part of the Community that forms at each table and of the larger weekend Community. Avoid dominating any situation or discussion. Let the pilgrims come to their own conclusions. On the other hand, do participate in developing summaries and in preparing posters.

Observe the following:

Who does the most talking?
Who talks least?
Who interprets what the group is saying?
Who dominates?

Try not to let one person dominate. Bring out the quiet ones by asking their opinion of the discussion topic. Avoid putting them on the spot.

If you have a disruptive person at the table, you may have to take that person aside and have a talk. Feel free to ask for help from the leaders' table. Prayers bring miracles.

Do not manipulate the pilgrims. The weekend will flow naturally. Do not expect the pilgrims act in a way that they would not do choose of their own accord. This may include raising hands, hugging strangers, speaking aloud in group prayer, and so on.

Keep the discussions moving; do not let them lag.

Posters and other creative expressions are a group effort. Let the ideas surface from among the group, and encourage all to participate.

Never leave the pilgrims alone at the table. Always stay at the table if one pilgrim is there.

Encourage the pilgrims to take notes, and take notes yourself.

Do not argue about theological differences. Ask the Spiritual Director to discuss these matters with the pilgrims in private.

If you have a clergy pilgrim at your table, do not direct all questions to him or her, and do not let the pilgrims address all the questions to the clergyperson. The opinions and responses of each group member are important.

Be an example of what is expected from each person on the weekend. Respond immediately to the bell; be prompt and on time!

Keep your appearance fresh. Smile and do not yawn.

Pray for the people at your table and for yourself.

Take no false pride in the fact that you have been on a Walk to Emmaus before. Do not talk about it unless asked and, if asked, tell the truth briefly and emphasize that this walk is for these pilgrims.

The Table Leader always sits with his or her back to the speaker and watches the pilgrims, noting facial expressions or gestures of lack of understanding related to a specific point in the talk.

THE DYNAMICS OF THE SMALL GROUP YOU ARE LEADING

The activities at each table in large part govern the success of the weekend for the pilgrims and ensure that the tables become cohesive groups. Many of the weekend activities center about the table. You are instrumental in the direction of these activities and their results. Success depends on how you transmit your thoughts and directions to the group and how you receive their thoughts and reactions.

Transmitting

Your role in directing the group:

Suggest new ideas; raise questions that further the discussion.

Try to clarify the meaning of various suggestions.

Think of results and difficulties no one else has perceived.

Summarize and get the group back to the subject; pull related suggestions together.

Analysis and Fact-Seeking

Your role in drawing out the group:

Ask questions to bring out fine points; get below the surface.

Rather than making statements, ask questions that bring out pertinent facts.

Think of questions or situations to highlight the knowledge and experience of others in the group.

Increasing Group Unity and Progress

Help your group practice the following:

Give honest encouragement.

Keep an open mind and help others to modify their viewpoints in light of contrasting views.

Find ways to reconcile clashing viewpoints.

Suppress the desire to criticize anyone in the group.

Encourage the pilgrims to develop better and faster thinking and responses.

Receiving

Your role in hearing and responding to the group:

Nod your head slightly—and wait.

Look at the speaker expectantly but do nothing and say nothing.

Use casual and noncommittal remarks: "I see," "Uh-huh," "Is that so?," and "That's interesting."

Repeat the last few words of the speaker.

Reflect to the speaker your understanding of what he or she has just said. Respond with a question.

When do you transmit and when do you receive—and how?

Each of these pointers helps you do a better job. For example, facts and suggestions that have little bearing on the topic may bog down the discussion. Somebody must get it back on topic. This is your job. At this point, you break in and redirect the discussion. In addition, you prod the quiet pilgrims and strengthen those who appear to lack confidence.

You also serve as a diplomat—a boss without showing it—planning, controlling, directing, and guiding primarily by asking questions. You stimulate, educate, facilitate, balance, and share control.

You see to it that everyone in the group participates in thinking, forming ideas and opinions, and making decisions. As group members begin to participate, they begin to control themselves, evaluate themselves as a group, and become responsible for the thoughts they are developing.

OPEN AND CLOSED QUESTIONS

As a Table Leader, ask open questions rather than closed ones. Open questions further thought and discussion.

Closed questions are those that people can answer with yes or no. Closed questions often begin with the words *is, do, has, can, will, shall.*

Open questions cannot be answered yes or no. For example: "How do you feel about this?" Open questions usually begin with the words *what, when, how, who, where, which.*

Respond as You Listen

A listening response is a brief comment or action that conveys the idea to someone without your attention and interest interfering with the speaker's train of thought. It normally occurs when the speaker pauses. It is not a time for you to insert your ideas, even if they support the speaker's thoughts. Allow the speaker to continue uninterrupted.

Questions That Draw and Involve

Frame questions in ways that encourage those who haven't actively participated in the discussion. Such questions usually follow a time when a few pilgrims have controlled discussions. If poorly expressed, these questions put the silent pilgrims on the spot or offend active pilgrims. If well framed, they open the discussion with no strain.

For example: "Do the rest of you agree with that?"—CLOSED question

"What do some of the rest of you think?"—OPEN question

Observe communication and learning styles of the table group members.

THE SUMMARY

The summary brings the discussion to a successful conclusion, and the thought processes and results of the discussion come into focus. If handled well, the main points stand out clearly and distinctly. As the table leader, you guide the table group to a point where the members draw a conclusion and express it in a summary statement.

KEEPING THE FIFTEEN TALKS ON SCHEDULE

Below are the key points of each of the fifteen talks. You may want to review these each morning and at noon, and make a few notes about the talks that will follow during that part of the day. Your notes can help you to keep the discussion for each talk moving in the proper direction. Please remember to keep your notes out of sight or mixed in with the notes that you will take during the talks. Don't be obvious about using them.

KEY POINTS OF ALL FIFTEEN TALKS

PRIORITY: Some basic differences distinguish humans from the rest of created order. Humans can set priorities and thus choose an ideal, informed by reason, for their life.

* The created order—three classifications (plants, animals, minerals).
* Definition of *priority*—something of leading importance in one's life; what one lives for; the shaping value for one's life.
* The capacity to make decisions and set priorities distinguishes humans from animals, plants, and minerals.
* Discover your priorities—material possessions, money, time?

PREVENIENT GRACE: God loves us and offers a relationship.

* The nature of God is infinitely creative, loving, and good.

Permission is granted to duplicate this page.

- The human situation—created in God's image, fallen from grace through sin, offered salvation in the reconciling work of Jesus Christ.

- God loves us and desires a relationship with us—even more than we desire a relationship with God.

- Definition of *prevenient grace*—God's love pursuing us, awakening and convincing us to come home.

- The loving acts of others communicate God's love to us.

- Personal statement by presenter on how he or she became aware of God's love.

PRIESTHOOD OF ALL BELIEVERS: All believers—laity and clergy alike—are called and given authority to be priests to one another.

- The world does not live in God's grace.

- The answer to the needs of the world is the salvation offered in Jesus Christ.

- Definition of *priesthood of all believers*—A priest acts as God's representative to persons in the world.

- The church consists of people who have experienced God's love and grace and want to share it with others.

- Personal statement by presenter about her or his own experience related to functioning as God's representative to the world.

Permission is granted to duplicate this page.

JUSTIFYING GRACE: The kind of grace at work when we honestly accept the relationship God offers us.

- We all have failed to respond to God's call to place our faith in Jesus Christ alone.

- We are justified when we say yes to the acceptance God offers through Christ: Christ died for us while we were yet sinners.

- The experience of justifying grace is also known as conversion, new birth, being born again, saved from sin, or being born of the Spirit.

- Salvation is both instantaneous and progressive, like two sides of a coin. It involves both justifying grace and sanctifying grace (the topic of the final grace talk).

- Justifying grace enables us to give our hearts to God.

- Personal statement by presenter about his/her own experience of justifying grace.

LIFE OF PIETY: A life lived in relationship with God.

- Definition of life of piety.

- Prayer is the language we use to communicate with God and to express our relationship with God.

- Scripture provides us with knowledge about the mind, heart, and will of God.

- Characteristics of a life of piety: attention, honesty, authenticity, communication, and resourcefulness.

- Important spiritual practices: prayer, scripture reading, meditation, worship, Communion, and spiritual direction.

- A life of piety has visible qualities that attract others to this kind of life. Such a life is not pious but reflects an awareness of ourselves, others, creation, and God; a desire to fulfill the relationship with God; action (which bears fruit in our decisions and lifestyle); direction (focused on Christ); naturalness (being ourselves); courage; and joy.

- Personal statement by presenter about her or his own experience of living the life of piety.

Permission is granted to duplicate this page.

GROW THROUGH STUDY: Study promotes our movement closer to the realization of Jesus as the model for our lives.

- Definition of *study*—an act or process by which we acquire knowledge of a subject for living. It is not simply an intellectual exercise but a discipline and willingness to inform our desires, emotions, and intuition about the Christian life. The purpose of study is to transform life through the renewal of the mind. (See Romans 12:2.)
- We are either growing or dying. Study helps us continue to grow.
- For a proper perspective, Christians study scripture to know God; we must also study ourselves, others, and the world we live in.
- Both obstacles and aids to study exist.
- The presenter describes his or her own style of study.

MEANS OF GRACE: The sacramental moments in our lives and the ways we corporately celebrate God's grace.

- The sacraments are those acts of worship, instituted by Christ, in which Christ is represented to us in such a way that we experience his presence anew in our lives.
- All Christian traditions recognize baptism and Holy Communion as sacraments.
- Other means of grace include the sacred moments in which Christ is made real for us through symbolic action or ritual at critical points in our lives.
- By grace through faith the Holy Spirit renews our spirits through each and every means of grace.
- Personal statement by presenter about her or his own experience of God's grace through one means of grace.

CHRISTIAN ACTION: Characterizes a Christ-centered life and flows from a relationship with Christ. Christian action bears witness to Christ and carries on his work in all we say and do.

- Definition of Christian action.
- This process begins when individual lives become Christ-centered.
- We give our hearts to Christ (piety); we give our minds to Christ (study); and we give our hands and feet to Christ (action).
- Christian action is a natural response to God's grace.
- Each person needs a plan of Christian action that starts with friendship.
- Personal statement by presenter about her or his own plan of action.

Permission is granted to duplicate this page.

OBSTACLES TO GRACE: Barriers to a relationship with God; any part of life being presented as the whole.

- Sin is pretending that we are the center of the universe.
- We can overcome sin by practicing the presence of God.
- We put our trust God to overcome obstacles to grace.
- The cross of Christ offers the key to overcoming the obstacles to our relationship with God (vertical) and with our neighbor (horizontal).
- Personal statement by presenter about her or his own experience of overcoming obstacles to grace.

DISCIPLESHIP: Responding fully to the relationship God offers by devoting our life to Christ.

- Serious Christians do not stop short of becoming a disciple.
- Discipleship involves giving our life totally to Christ.
- Disciples seek to glorify God in all they do—with head, heart, and hands.
- Disciples demonstrate these natural qualities: understands priority, has discipline, knows reality, shows empathy, takes initiative, and practices generosity.
- Disciples demonstrate these spiritual qualities: a lively faith, humility, hope, and love.
- Personal statement by presenter about her or his own experience of accountable discipleship.

CHANGING OUR WORLD: Looking at the natural environment and deciding on a plan of action to bring the world to Christ.

- Our first field of ministry is ourselves. Prayer, study, and action change us.
- In the second field of ministry, we bring others to Christ and the church (through prayer, study, and action).
- The third field of ministry is our city, state, and nation (through prayer, study, and action).
- The fourth field of ministry is the other people and nations of the world (through prayer, study, and action).
- Personal statement by presenter of his or her plan of action for each field of ministry.

Permission is granted to duplicate this page.

SANCTIFYING GRACE: The work of the Holy Spirit moves us toward perfection in love and truth.

- Sanctifying grace is the work of the Holy Spirit in rooting out sin—moving us from *imputed* righteousness (what Christ did for us) to *imparted* righteousness (what Christ does in us).

- Definition of sanctifying grace: the process by which the Holy Spirit reveals to us the original righteousness.

- The Holy Spirit indwells and empowers us to love as God loves.

- Sanctifying grace empowers our entire ministry.

- Because God is infinite, our opportunities to grow in grace are also infinite.

- Personal statement by presenter about the work of sanctifying grace in her or his own life.

BODY OF CHRIST: In this talk, pilgrims will come to understand how the church can empower them to be Christ's representatives in the world to the "least of these."

- The primary reason for Emmaus is to strengthen local churches and to develop strong ecumenical leadership in order to fulfill the Great Commission.

- Definition of *body of Christ*: the entire Christian community in mission to the world.

- The body of Christ must utilize the gifts of all its members to fulfill its mission.

- Characteristics of the body of Christ: alive and life-giving, equipping, intentional in witness, humble in service, confident in Christ's final victory.

- We all need to develop a plan for action that reaches out to the "least of these."

- Personal statement by presenter of how the church has empowered her or him to be Christ's representative in the world.

Permission is granted to duplicate this page.

PERSEVERANCE: This talk explains the need for follow-up and the follow-up system of the Emmaus Community (the group reunion and reunion cards).

- Definition of *perseverance*: Continuing to act in the face of difficulty and opposition; to be steadfast in purpose; to press on in the life of grace.

- Pilgrims need to maintain contact with Christ and other Christians.

- The weekly meeting of the group reunion is the premium we pay to persevere in a life of grace.

- Explain group reunions, reunion cards, monthly Gatherings, and Emmaus teams.

- Personal testimony of perseverance by the speaker.

FOURTH DAY: Continues the idea of perseverance in that each succeeding day will be a "fourth day"—every day hereafter for the rest of your life.

- We have experienced God's grace through gifts and sacrifices of the Emmaus Community.

- Our mission now becomes bringing others into a deeper relationship with Christ.

- Pilgrims are sent from the Walk into the world to become a part of the revelation of God's reign. This journey is one of spiritual growth in grace and full participation in God's mission.

- Two dangers: (a) believing you are someone special, and (b) believing you are a nobody.

- We maintain contact with Christ and others, knowing and keeping our priority.

- Personal statement by the speaker of her or his Fourth Day experience.

Permission is granted to duplicate this page.

 **APPENDICES**

APPENDIX A

TEAM MEETINGS

Team members become a genuine team through an intentional period of team formation. Team formation occurs during a series of well-planned team meetings that involve both lay and clergy team members. Throughout the process, team members prepare and grow together to become God's hands and feet during the event.

Reasons for Team Formation

An intentional team formation process is essential to fulfilling the goals of the Emmaus movement:

1. *To prepare team members functionally.* Through team meetings, all team members prepare themselves for their responsibilities on the event. Rehearsing talks and responsibilities during team meetings releases anxiety. Practicing also reassures team members that God is indeed present and will be powerfully present on the event. Furthermore, team members have a chance to work through their own responses to talks ahead of time so they can be more attentive to the pilgrims' responses during the event.

2. *To prepare team members spiritually.* The event team leaders attempt to make each person's experience on the team a spiritual exercise and an opportunity for spiritual growth. For example, each talk gives its presenter an opportunity to grow both in understanding and in practicing the topic of the talk. Team meetings offer occasions to encourage team members to put their spiritual lives in order, to remember who and whose they are, and to reflect upon God's call to this ministry. The meetings foster the renewal of the practices of piety, study, and action.

3. *To build a spirit of Christian community.* The leadership for these events is not a group of individuals carrying out assigned tasks but a *team* of people who are becoming a Christian community. This Community provides the caring environment in which the pilgrims come to live for a time. Each aspect of team meetings—worship, sharing, team education, talk

previews, prayer—works toward providing a bonding experience for team members. The team moves from being strangers to being friends in Christ; people who know and care about one another, who appreciate one another's strengths and weaknesses. The event team leaders' most significant work is the preparation and building of the team.

4. *To train leaders for future events.* Team formation is a primary way people learn about Emmaus Ministries events and how they are led. Through the hands-on experience of team meetings, the team leaders pass on the common wisdom of the Emmaus movement to newer members of the Community and cultivate new leaders. If the team leaders neglect team formation, the Community will never develop new leaders who are well-grounded in the purpose and procedures of the movement.

5. *To develop Christian leaders for work outside the Community.* The importance of team formation resides in the Community's purpose beyond simply carrying out events: the development of Christian maturity and leadership. Team participation helps form individuals as Christians and as spiritual leaders. Team members cultivate the practical and spiritual skills to become Christian leaders in their church and community. Members exercise their individual gifts during team meetings and focus their energies on service to God. They learn to: articulate their faith through talk preparation; pray together and intercede for others; gently lead a group in discussing deep and sensitive subjects; maintain a humble, servant attitude; live in community; work as a team; actively listen to people; and pay attention to God's presence amid human interaction.

Participation at Team Meetings

It is essential that team members participate in the entire team process. Those contacting prospective team members tell them of the expected commitment. In many communities, a general rule of thumb is that team members participate in at least three-fourths of the total number of team meetings. Many active persons have difficulty scheduling around family, school, work, and church obligations. Nevertheless, the formation of a team requires that team members commit time to team meetings.

Clergy team members are expected to participate in team meetings as well. The Spiritual Director sets the example by committing to attend all team meetings and previewing the talks. The team needs to build rapport with the clergy, and all team members will benefit from their spiritual guidance before the event.

Team meetings involve only the Conference Room Team: Those who will be in the conference room with the pilgrims for the entire event. Though support persons working behind the scenes are an integral part of the event, team meeting attendance will not directly help them perform their duties. Involving support persons in team meetings may unnecessarily overextend these servants.

Agenda for a Team Meeting

Team meetings generally consist of several elements:

- **Worshiping together** at the beginning of each meeting. Lay and clergy team members can rotate leadership for this time of worship or Communion.

- **Sharing our spiritual lives** in "floating" group reunions. For a few minutes after worship, the event team leader may invite pilgrims to gather in groups of two or three to respond to a question or two from the group reunion card or other questions the event team leaders choose. This sharing fosters team relationships, focuses the team on the spiritual life, and readies the team inwardly for the remainder of the meeting.

- **Developing a thorough understanding of Emmaus.** For a few minutes at each meeting, an event team leader expands team members' understanding of the ministry by reviewing one aspect of the program and the team's responsibilities. The *Team Manual* may be used for this purpose, with the team reading an assigned portion that is then reviewed at the subsequent meeting.

- **Helping one another prepare** for and practice the tasks: talk previews, table leadership, and music leadership.

- **Praying together** at the close of the meeting and throughout team formation. Prayer undergirds and empowers each event from beginning to end, including the prayers of the team throughout team formation. Praying for one another extends God's love to another and binds the team together as a family of God. In addition to taking time at each meeting to pray corporately, team members are each assigned a prayer partner for whom he or she prays through the duration of team formation.

Team meetings are not the place to work out details of buying food, organizing food or acts of agape, deciding whom to assign for this or that, and so on. These responsibilities belong to specific persons who do their work outside of team meetings. The event lay team leader and the assistants will meet separately from team meetings to ensure that support needs are being handled. Good planning and wise use of team meeting time fosters positive team morale and confidence in the team leaders.

Furthermore, team meetings do not consist of a series of tasks for completion so everyone can get home. The primary purpose of team meetings is building the team. Even when meetings wrap up early the event lay team leader will make use of the remaining time to build relationships, skills, and a servant attitude.

Previewing Talks

All speakers—lay and clergy alike—present their talk to the team just as they will present the talk at the event. This gives the speakers the chance to practice the talk and gain strength from the team's affirmation and suggestions for improvements. No one is above improvement, and the team offers suggestions in an atmosphere of care and affirmation. Previewing the talks underscores the fact that each speaker depends upon the others to convey the total message of the event. When a team member presents a talk and receives the team's comments, the talk no longer belongs just to that speaker but to the entire team. The Spiritual Director takes an active role in talk previews to ensure theological soundness, clarity, and relevance to real life. The Spiritual Director meets with those having trouble pulling their talks together.

No speaker surprises the team on the Walk with a radically different talk than the one previewed without consulting the Lay Director and/or Spiritual Director. A person who refuses to share his or her talk with the team before the Walk chooses not to be a team member.

Before each speaker previews his or her talk, the Lay Director asks the speaker's team prayer partner or another team member to pray aloud for the speaker. The group, under the leadership of the Music Director, sings the appropriate traditional song as determined by the Board of Directors (such as "Sing Hallelujah")

Then the Assistant Lay Director makes the "With a clean sheet of paper. . . ." introduction, and the speaker leads the group in the Prayer to the Holy Spirit. The speaker then introduces the talk; writes the title of the talk and his or her name on the board, displays a piece of poster board with the title written on it, or has someone project a visual on a screen; presents the talk using any planned visual aids; concludes the talk by saying "Amen" or "De Colores" and leaves the room. For the PRIORITY talk, the speaker does not use the Prayer to the Holy Spirit and does not end the talk with "Amen" or "De Colores." Each speaker prepares to present the finished talk before the team just as though presenting on the Walk.

Team members review the talk by listening for the main points of the talk outline, considering the speaker's success at bringing fundamental points to life with illustration or personal witness, and noting any obstacles to communication in the speaker's content or style. The Lay Director gives team members copies of "Key Points of Talks" listed below or from the *Walk to Emmaus Team Manual* to aid in evaluation. To maintain consistent quality and content of each Walk, each speaker needs to cover the main points of his or her talk.

When the speaker finishes and leaves the room for the chapel, the Lay Director forms simulated table groups and asks the team members to review the talk by reflecting upon at least these two questions:

1. What about this talk can you affirm?
2. How can this talk still be improved?

The team receives a few moments of silence to reflect upon the talk in light of these questions and then members share their reflections in the small groups. Table Leaders take turns leading the group discussion, commenting on the first question before moving to the second. After ten minutes of discussion, the Lay Director calls the speaker back into the room to receive from each Table Leader the affirmations and suggestions for improvement. Once a statement or suggestion has surfaced, groups do not need to repeat it. Following the table reports, the Lay Director opens the floor for other comments and clarifications.

The talk preview affords an indispensable opportunity for team members to learn to speak the truth in love with one another. The Lay and Spiritual Directors foster an atmosphere of caring and affirmation that cuts off insensitive and unnecessary criticism while challenging each speaker with the truth about needed improvements. The Spiritual Director actively participates in talk previews to ensure theological soundness, clarity, and relevance to life and stands ready to meet with team members who face difficulties pulling their talks together.

Preparing Table Leaders and Assistant Table leaders

The Table Leader holds the most influential job in the conference room. A Table Leader can make all the difference in a person's experience of the event, for better or for worse. So, Table Leaders deserve sufficient orientation and training for their role.

Here are some helpful resources.

- Talk preview discussions in small groups during team meetings can provide the opportunity for team members to practice guiding a small-group discussion.

- A well-planned team discussion on the role of the Table Leader and on keys to effective table leadership can elicit a wealth of insight from team members on helpful table leadership.

- A Table Leader/Assistant Table Leader training workshop that includes presentation, discussion, and role play during a team meeting can be a valuable tool. Teams for a pair of Walks come together for one hour (assuming the teams meet simultaneously). This workshop is available in Appendix D.

- This *Team Manual* devotes a chapter to table leadership. Every Table Leader and Assistant Table Leader will study and discuss this chapter during team training.

- Duplicate and distribute copies of "The Importance of the Table Leader" (from the "Team Meeting Forms and Handouts" section) to remind Table Leaders of their responsibilities and the necessary leadership style.

Preparing Music Directors

Music Directors can prepare themselves and the team by leading music during team meetings and teaching the members songs necessary to the event. Worship times during team meetings offer occasions to try out special music for the event. A brief discussion on team members' experiences of good music leadership can encourage and strengthen Music Directors. In addition, every Music Director will have in hand the Music Director's Checklist (see the "Music Directors" section in *The Walk to Emmaus Directors' Manual*) and be prepared to share the traditions behind "De Colores" and the singing of grace before and after meals. The event team leaders meet with the Music Leaders to make sure they share common expectations for the Music Leaders roles during the event and to plan for music on the event.

Team Meeting Schedules

Before the first team meeting, the Board of Directors conducts an orientation that covers team responsibilities, support committee responsibilities, an overview of Emmaus, and the plan for team formation. After the final team meeting, a potluck fellowship with spouses may be held. This meeting could include a commissioning service, Communion, and last-minute reminders.

Team-formation schedules need to include enough hours to preview all the talks and build the team. This number derives from the various elements to be accomplished: worship, group reunions and team building, training on specific topics, talk previews, and prayer time. Each Community works out a schedule that best suits its situation in order to fulfill the goals of team formation. For a full-length Walk to Emmaus, one of the following schedules may be useful.

- *Eight to ten weekly meetings.* This schedule employs weekly meetings of approximately three hours each. This plan especially suits Communities in which team members live, work, or attend school close enough to one another to make weekly evening meetings possible. An extended number of meetings gives the team time to grow together gradually. This schedule also gives the event team leaders plenty of time to notice and respond to needs among the team members.

- *Four biweekly or monthly meetings.* This schedule consists of four all-day meetings of about six hours each. This schedule especially suits Communities in which team members must drive long distances to meetings, which makes successive weekly and evening meetings difficult. This schedule requires four talk previews for each meeting (one meeting will have three talk previews. Seasoned team members can preview their talks at the first meeting to serve as a model for new team members. Other than requiring the preview of more talks at each meeting, the elements of each session follow the description above.

- *Two Friday evening and all-day Saturday meetings.* This schedule consists of two meetings each starting on Friday evening and ending on Saturday evening (meeting hours would be roughly 7–10 p.m. on Friday, and 9 a.m.–5 p.m. on Saturday). Each meeting may require that some team members spend the night. The team members living close enough to go home Friday night could graciously host those who cannot return home overnight. This schedule again provides all the elements of the team meetings. To make better use of the available time, make meal arrangements in advance.

APPENDIX B

CRITIQUE SHEET FOR TALK PREVIEWS

Listen and watch for the following during talk previews. Remember to present all critiques in love and affirmation.

What about this talk can you affirm?

How can this talk still be improved?

Length of talk _____

Presentation
    Words that may present a problem
    Are the witness and stories appropriate to the topic?
    Vocal inflections
        Too soft
        Too loud
        Too slow
        Too fast
RED-FLAG ISSUES
    Naming:
        Church
        Person
        Political stance
        Issues of the church
DISTRACTIONS
    Mannerisms
        Facial expressions
        Eye contact
        Hand gestures
        Moving about
    Jewelry

    Attire
        The speaker dresses to reinforce the value of this talk.
        Men—suit (or sport coat) and tie
        Women—dress or suit

Speakers may wear their Emmaus cross during the talk, but they do not wear the cross after that until the cross ceremony.

Scripture references
    Appropriate to the topic
    Sufficient
    Not too many
Speed of delivery
    Too fast for people to take notes?
Visuals
    Easy to read across the room
    Not cluttered
Clergy
    Talking, not preaching
Handouts
    Only a list of scripture verses in the closing packet
    The pilgrims rely on their notes: the items God moves them to remember

Permission is granted to copy this page for team meeting talk previews only.

APPENDIX C

HANDOUTS

The Emmaus model does not involve handouts for Emmaus talks. Many speakers believe handouts help the pilgrims discern the crucial aspects of the talks.

The Emmaus design provides an experiential event for the pilgrims. For this, the pilgrims take notes as led by the Holy Spirit. The pilgrims record the information they deem important, not what the speaker thinks the pilgrims should note. If each speaker provided three hand-outs, each pilgrim would receive 45 handouts. The likelihood of a pilgrim sorting through a stack of handouts is slim. The pilgrim is more apt to review his or her personal notes rather than handouts.

A brief list of scripture references from the fifteen talks may be prepared and provided in the closing packet.

APPENDIX D

TABLE TRAINING

Table training for Emmaus encompasses many aspects. Being an effective Table Leader or Assistant Table Leader requires preparation. The pilgrims will spend about one-third of the seventy-two hours in the table environment, about one-half the waking hours of the event.

This material offers an approach to table training for Emmaus. The weekend Lay and Spiritual Directors or a group of Community trainers (former weekend Lay and Spiritual Directors) may conduct this training.

Items Needed:

Three large round tables
Eight chairs at each table
Writing materials on each table
Marker board and markers
Lectern

Getting Started

Seat the six Table Leaders together with one Assistant Lay Director and one Assistant Spiritual Director. Seat the six Assistant Table Leaders at the second table with one Assistant Lay Director and one Assistant Spiritual Director. The third table hosts the three Music Directors, the Board Representative, the remaining two Assistant Spiritual Directors and the other Assistant Lay Director. The participation of all the team members offers several advantages:

- Helps build team and community;

- Enhances team response since all team members will interact with the pilgrims;

- Provides for back-up training in the case of an emergency;

- Gives an avenue of encouragement to the team members who will not be at the tables with the pilgrims;

- Promotes the servanthood atmosphere of the team;

- Fosters leadership development.

The weekend Lay and Spiritual Directors provide a brief overview of the training.

Getting in Touch with Feelings (about a 10-Minute Talk)

Suggested scripture: Luke 22:24-27
Consider using John 3:30 to close the talk.
The trainer does the following:

- Emphasizes servanthood as a style of leadership;

- Affirms team members' feelings of anxiety and apprehension;
- Focuses on the feelings of the pilgrims;
- Relates personal feelings in joining a table group on his or her Walk.

Each table group forms two smaller groups (about six to seven-minute exercise)
Small-group members share their feelings about joining a table group.

- Do not judge others' feelings.
- Affirm one another.
- Concentrate on your own feelings.

The table groups reassemble (about ten minutes).
Each table group jointly prepares a written summary of the small-group sharing.

Each table group reports its summary to the team (five to six minutes).

Trainers respond to the reports (five minutes).

Discussion of Table Dynamics (by Trainers)

Table Leaders have the unique task of guiding a group of strangers into an experience of community. The success of the weekend for the pilgrims, to a large extent, depends on what happens at the table.

Table Leaders are instrumental in directing the activities at the table and in building family around the table.

Table Leaders do the following:

- Provide structure and limits for the group in an atmosphere of love;
- Provide an atmosphere of acceptance and caring;
- Help the members become independent;
- Help the members develop interdependence;
- Help the members become self-directed.

Table Leaders help each person feel at home, comfortable, at ease.
The musical *Oliver*
Oliver is alone and asks, "Where is love?"
Gradually from all around, voices speak these words:
"Consider yourself at home;
Consider yourself one of the family."
Table Leaders foster a climate and atmosphere that helps people desire a closer walk with Jesus Christ.
Table Leaders do not anticipate the pilgrims' reactions.

- Each pilgrim discovers the meaning of the weekend for himself or herself.

- Bear witness to your belief in Jesus Christ.
- Let the pilgrims learn by experience.
- Remember, this is not your weekend.
- You are a servant.

Table Leaders

- Foster a loving, trusting environment in which the pilgrims can grow.

  Lead pilgrims into their own discoveries. Pilgrims leave on Sunday, strengthened by the renewed faith they have discovered for themselves.

  Provide an environment in which God can work.

- Avoid arguments about differences in theology.

  Argument involves winning or losing; Emmaus fosters discovery for the individual.

- Communicate love and acceptance to your group.

  Groups, like individuals, respond to praise and encouragement.

  Affirm the group.

  Affirm the individuals.

  Get to know each pilgrim at your table.

  Personal contact is important; spend each mealtime with a different individual. Share in a way that is comfortable and natural.

- Set standards and provide limits. Do this in love.

  Gently remind the group of its tasks.

  Intervene when someone is

  > being hurt;
  >
  > blocking;
  >
  > dominating;
  >
  > judging.

  Watch and listen for the for following:

  > Who does the most talking?
  >
  > Who talks the least?
  >
  > Who interprets what the group is saying?
  >
  > Who dominates?

- Avoid putting anyone on the spot.

  Take persons aside to talk.

  Ask for help from the Lay and/or Spiritual Director.

  Keep the discussion moving; don't let it lag.

Silence can be helpful.

- Remember that table activities are group efforts. The pilgrims provide the ideas for posters or talk representations. Guide them in note taking.

- Affirm individuals within the group; that affirmation helps to develop community.

- Encourage the involvement of all.

- Help the group members assume an increasing share of responsibility and leadership for the table activities.

  Do not let the group become dependent on you.

  Letting go is an important part of leadership.

APPENDIX E

TABLE NAMES FOR WALKS

Men's Walks	Women's Walks
Matthew	*Sarah*
Mark	*Anna*
Luke	*Esther*
John	*Martha*
Paul	*Mary*
Peter	*Naomi*
Thomas	*Ruth*

APPENDIX F

THEMES ACROSS THE DAYS

The first talk of each day focuses on the decisions we need to make.

PRIORITY

What will I do with my life?

GROW THROUGH STUDY

On what or whom will I base my life?

CHANGING OUR WORLD

What difference do I want to make in this world?

The second talk focuses on the theme of that day.

PREVENIENT GRACE

God's grace envelops us.

MEANS OF GRACE

Ways I receive and live in grace.

SANCTIFYING GRACE

Ways I can grow toward holiness and embody grace.

The third talk focuses on the ways Christians serve.

PRIESTHOOD OF ALL BELIEVERS

Sharing grace with others.

CHRISTIAN ACTION

Sharing Christ with others.

BODY OF CHRIST

Sharing with all members of the Christian community in the ministry and mission of Christ.

The fourth talk focuses on individual responses to the themes.

JUSTIFYING GRACE

How do you respond to God's grace? (I accept.)

OBSTACLES TO GRACE

How do you respond to impediments to a life of grace? (Sometimes I stand, sometimes I fall; always I take up the cross.)

PERSEVERANCE

What will you do to continue living in grace? (Participate regularly in group reunions, Gatherings, the local church, and global missions.)

The fifth talk focuses on our lifestyle.

LIFE OF PIETY

Living a life of devotion to God.

DISCIPLESHIP

Committing to being Christ in the church and world.

FOURTH DAY

Persevering in grace.

Permission is granted to duplicate this page.